*Letters*
*from the*
*Takeaway*

# Khaled Hakim

# *Letters from the Takeaway*

## *and*
## *Other*
## *Distances*

Shearsman Books

First published in the United Kingdom in 2019 by
Shearsman Books
50 Westons Hill Drive
Emersons Green
BRISTOL
BS16 7DF

Shearsman Books Ltd Registered Office
30–31 St. James Place, Mangotsfield, Bristol BS16 9JB
*(this address not for correspondence)*

www.shearsman.com

ISBN 978-1-84861-637-0

# Contents

to the Preserver

# Foreword

## Tim Atkins

Khaled Hakim. (a) We loved him, and (b) he pissed everybody off most of the time, all of the time[1]. Long before he became a famous poet, according to legend, he ran away from home in Birmingham and washed up in New York's lower east side, alternating between the Poetry Project at St Mark's Place and the kitchens of a family-owned Avenue A curry house[2]. Every time he appeared at a poetry event in the mid-1990s he insisted on telling people that he didn't know who he was or what he was doing there, and half of the time, we believed him. Back in the days when Miles Champion & Caroline Bergvall were slim young poetry groovers upon whom everybody's poetry hopes rode for the possibility of a non-combative, body-odour-free, and sexy new poetry, Khaled was the great, glowering, anti-hero whose twerking stirred up and excited the 37 writers who comprised the British mid-nineties dirty white experimental poetry pantomime.

The scene, back then, revolved around readings organized by Drake Stutesman & Thomas Evans[3] at the East West Gallery in Ladbroke Grove, and somewhat latterly, at readings organized by Miles Champion[4] & myself[5] at the Platform Gallery off Brick Lane.[6] (Mike Diss – a lovely man – also ran a series called Vertical Images. He now appears to be a psychotherapist in Walthamstow). It's hard to imagine, these days, how few events there were for poets under 40. It's even more unimaginable to

---

[1] make sure y/ rite loads (all footnotes from an email from K.H. *Some Pointers for My Forrword*)

[2] Make sur yoo tell them I was Asian befor Asians wer invented

[3] Mak sure y/ tel them I saved Tomas from a drunken rapist

[4] mak sure yu tell them how i deliverd Milezs first born on th back of a milk flote

[5] make sure y/ tel them how i deliverd yr first born in a tomata greenhose

[6] tell them I delivered Tomases first born on a skatbord in Longleet safari

imagine how few poets there were – at all – who were reading L=A=N=G=U=A=G=E poetry and who were familiar with *any* non-British innovative poetries. Karlein van den Beukel & Dell Olson were happily active, Caroline Bergvall was in Dartington (THREE women – heavens!) and there were no poets on the scene who weren't middle class and white. In a way, this was understandable – for however much we wanted an open and expansive milieu for poets of all shapes & sizes, skin colours & sexualities, it would have almost certainly seemed a closed-off and forbidding space. For Khaled, I think that this was part of its gruesome attraction.[7]

When Khaled appeared in the mid-90s, presenting himself as a Paki/Brummie/Auteur/Filmmaker (his words – he is the only person who I have ever heard use the word "Paki"[8]) his work was a source of enormous excitement. (He's always reminded me of Kevin Rowland in his manias and popular appeal, but that's another story). You get the poetry in this volume, of course, and it, to my mind, mirrors the man himself very closely. Both are full of contradiction. Part of the joy of reading Khaled's work is the way that the reader swings from enjoyment to amazement to outrage and surprise with every new line. It's like descending a high alpine peak on a hairpin road at top speed. The constant changes of direction maintain extremely high levels of excitement but you never know if the next turn is going to surprise you with a completely different perspective or throw you over the edge – and then there's the occasional urge to vomit. This is what you get with the poems and this is what, after midnight, in a poetry basement in east or west London in 1998, you might have got with the human.

To the best of my memory, Khaled was last sighted in the basement of The Platform Gallery in Brick Lane in the

---

[7] Tell them i saved British ptry from global warming & sliding off the Canford Cliffs
[8] tell them im the onlie black poet in the wld

autumn of 1999. He became immediately unobtainable and his rare & fugitive poetry publications dried up. He taught Sufi drumming somewhere in North London and the only reason that I know this is because I found a thumbnail picture and an advertisement in a community centre in about 2007 when I was trying to get back in touch. He didn't answer my emails for well over a decade, but that didn't stop me publishing some early poems in an edition of onedit.net. I've always read and adored his work. Khaled, in person, has *always* been a compelling and beautiful experience. And at bottom, of course, he has always been a long-gone, lost and lovable individual, banging on his bendir and dancing around the living-room like a beatnik old daddy.

I adore Khaled, of course, for all of these reasons. However nutty and confrontational he was (and he was), he was also hugely tender and vulnerable. As with many great poets (there – I've said it) there is the ability to hold and combine a great many contradictory impulses and thoughts. Part of Khaled always wanted everybody's approval (who doesn't?) and one way that he got this was by being a dazzling conversationalist who would dive into any conversation with passion, depth of knowledge, and strongly-held opinions. (He always said that he had no strongly-held opinions – *of course*). He always knew that his work and his background was a source of great attraction to a group of white liberal poets in a depressingly vanilla landscape, but (and there is always a but) I know that he also felt that his colour or class or accent was a source of exclusion. It's one of the major tropes of his poetry and came up constantly in his conversation. Did it make us feel uncomfortable? Well – yes – because we didn't feel or notice it half as much as he did (and of course we all yearned for this inclusivity) and part of Khaled's mission was to make us feel uncomfortable about our participation in such exclusionary practice. It is a practice which continues in much of the British avant-garde to this day. And so – a typical evening would run along the lines of Khaled being brilliant and being a fabulously unpredictable livewire, and would (depending on which way his wind was blowing) end in camaraderie and collective endeavour (we were all in the same room because of our shared love of poetry, after all) or in misunderstanding and division. As with all small groups of young poets there was always room for tiny personal or poetic differences to lead to large disagreements. Khaled's desire for approval was balanced by his disgust with himself at liking such bourgeois poetry and his need to have conversations with so many non-takeaway-type writers.[9]

One of Khaled's great tricks has been his ability to turn these profound and ongoing contradictions into such a finely performed poetry. It's the most honest and the most dishonest poetry that I know[10]. I suspect that Khaled knows he is a genius. I am sure that it pisses him off that the people who believe him to be such have very little cultural capital and don't have as much talent as him. Perhaps it annoys him that his creativity lies in a field where nobody is paying much attention[11]. I have no idea if he feels that he is paid attention by a vanilla audience because – as well as being a great writer – he's such an exotic and shiny old bird. I'd hazard a guess that at least some of his non-P.C. statements are made to prick the balloons of his perceived readers as opposed to being deeply-felt convictions. At times, I'm reminded of the feeling that I used to get when watching John Waters' movies; he's doing it to get a different kind of attention. I believe that he's also doing it to make us question our own positions and assumptions.

An introduction to a collection of long-forgotten and recently-discovered poems is the perfect place to make outrageous claims. Here goes: Khaled Hakim is the great lost

---

[9] tel them I was the onlie non wite w/in a 300 mile radius
[10] tell them im Bangladeshi i only look white
[11] tell them abowt my gurilla training

British experimental writer of the last quarter century[12]. I believe that his importance (which concerns me less than the pleasure that his work gives – but that's another story) lies in the fact that he brings a powerful and original set of ingredients to the most important kind of contemporary poetry. His filmmaking background and clear engagement with the work of Stan Brakhage changed the speed and the angle of his L=A=N=G=U=A=G=E-polarized poetry. He was the only UK poet to work with David Antin's conversational poetics. His Brummie-styled phonetic writing drew parallels with the similarly individual universes of Tom Leonard and bill bissett, and his class and colour were – and still are, of course – important.[13] The conversations that his writing and being sparked in the 1990s have never really been followed through in British poetry. Danez Smith, in a recent interview, stated that "British poetry is a decade or two behind America in terms of publishing people of colour and in the awards and in recognising the need for different gatekeepers." I'd say he's wrong. In terms of size and quality, it is a hundred years behind. Who knows what would have happened if Khaled hadn't disappeared into a box of floppy discs? The world would have been completely different. It would certainly have been bigger and it most probably would have been better.

Bernadette Mayer, as ever, says things best: *Wake up! The cobra commander is back. To make love, turn to page 27. To die, turn to…* whatever title they cook up for this kind-of-okay-for-a-middle-aged-Brummie's long lost floppy disc poetry collection. Look upon these works, ye mighty, and tremble.

Dr[14] Tim Atkins[15]

---

[12] make sure yu tell them you owe yr entier poetick career to playgiarizing my waste bin w/ my permission
[13] tel them about my gurilla
[14] mak sure yu sound qwalifyed
[15] Did i tell yoo im Asian?

# Acknowledgements

During a brief period in the '90s I allowed to be published less than a dozen poetic works – I can't be sure of the number or how it happened. I can't be sure of when they were written or what order. The last publication was in Nicholas Johnson's *Foil: defining poetry 1985-2000* which neatly closes the period. Indeed, I believe I never proofed those anthology pieces, left no forwarding address for copies, was uncontactable for the opening launch, and had already disappeared from the poetry world for the next fifteen years. That is pretty emblematic of my careless disregard, irritated observance, and ultimate ingratitude during a time that would leave me as scarcely a footnote in an already marginal activity.

That life got packed in boxes, and the unpublished works and drafts became anachronisms on floppy disks. And never another thought about it till about 2015. I opened a box, read some handwritten pages, couldn't remember writing them, but thought he had something whoever he was. I believed the majority of my work including the performative routines was inaccessible until someone told me that floppy disk readers were *cheap*.

When I put toes into the innovative poetry scene again in 2016, I was a nobody. I'm not sure I was anybody when I was active. For a mainly performative poet it felt like there wasn't a gig to be had for love nor money. Then I went to the Small Publishers Fair in Conway Hall and met four of my erstwhile publishers. Many thanks to Kelvin Corcoran, Andrew Duncan, Tony Frazer, and Nicholas Johnson for their time and encouragement since then.

I tell myself that I only bothered to put together the manuscripts for two books (this volume, and the forthcoming performance work, *The Routines 1983-2000*) because I was midwifing the birth of a very different work with a very different tenor – a 'degraded epic' that had taken over six years. The old work would clear a space for *Barzakh* to make a splash. But as I spent time with the older work it seemed a shame they'd spent so long in utter obscurity given that the project I was engaged in was so singularly aberrant.

Looking at the prosody of both the 'poems' and the performative work – both of which disdain the poetic for a hollowed-out discursiveness – I couldn't get a feel for what was originally behind it apart from dadaistic gesture. It took months before I remembered that it didn't owe anything to then-current poetics or individual poets because it was in reaction to the whole framework of poetry, and that the language I used to navigate with came from the artworld and experimental film-making.

Inevitably I am a stranger to these poems. Others gave them a home. Opening up that cardbox box marked 'Poetics' it contained letters and manuscripts from poets, invitations to publish: all I wager I left unanswered. I am being reminded of supposed conversations with publishers offering to do a book – I have no recollection and would have regarded it in the same manner as an invitation to join them at the gym.

I am grateful to that initial group of poet-supporters who congregated around the East West Gallery readings organized by Thomas Evans, and later platforms with Miles Champion and Karlien van den Beukel, whose faith I tried with my wildly uneven performance routines. It is to Thomas Evans I owe the most. He it was who first *got* me: the minimalist poetics and the ear behind it, particularly the performative work which is couched in fuck-off dumbness.

This year I have suddenly realized that 30 years ago I was the only non-white pebble on the UK experimental poetry shore. My poetics certainly played up 'non-bourgeois' tropes – the belligerence, the anti-intellectualism, the denial of sensitivity. But the damage and destructive tendencies that have brought me to invisibility are the same forces that led me to take up an occulted practice in the first place – one that cuts me off from much of my family and community.

I want to know if anything I did is relevant now. Only old people know me. But by temperament I am an adolescent autodidact who forged an occasional poetry of narrative, theory, and insult.

I am just starting out.

*Walthamstow 2018*

*Letter to Brakhage* was published both by Miles Champion, who wheedled it out of me for *Tongue to Boot* #3 (Summer 1996), and by Tim Atkins in *Onedit* #9. And I hear there are recordings of it in libraries. Written much earlier, as my first poem in this form, I am amazed I got it right first time. Stan kindly answered the letter.

*Letter to Antin* was picked up by Andrew Duncan for *Angel Exhaust* 14 (Winter 1996) and was also reproduced in *Foil*. David didn't answer the letter. The address to Nicholas Johnson at the beginning is anachronistic: Nicholas never saw it till it was going to *Foil*. But I owe him that much – I'm proud he thinks as highly of my work as he does and part of me thinks this book should have been amongst the voice-led Black Mountain-conscious poets of his Etruscan Books.

*Run Poem* was published as a chapbook for Kelvin Corcoran's Short Run series (Spring 1996) and was also reproduced in *Foil*.

*Second Letter to Brakhage* was circulated in manuscript and probably reached a wider readership than some published pieces. I thought it got formally published somewhere but I'm not sure. From internal evidence it's the earliest completed poem in this book.

*Second Letter from the Takeaway* is the *first* of my poems to be published, in *Angel Exhaust* 12 (Autumn 1995).

*Letter from the Takeaway 1 & Letter from the Takeaway 4* (as originally titled) were published in a double issue of *Talus* 9/10 (1997) guest-edited by Thomas Evans.

*Third Letter from the Takeaway* was published after my return to poetry, in *Shearsman* magazine 111/112 (Spring 2017).

*Letter to Peter Gidal/Kurt Kren* was originally presented at an East West reading as *Letter to Gidal*. I still regard it as primarily a performance piece, but there tends to be cross-over between textual and performative pieces. I believe it was originally unfinished.

*Ben-Hur* I thought was roughly contemporary with *Letter for S* but is probably earlier and got forgotten as I left poetry. It was published in *Shearsman* magazine 117/118 (Winter 2018), guest-edited by Kelvin Corcoran.

*Letter for S* was published in *Foil: Defining Poetry 1985-2000*, and aside from perhaps site-specific performances it is the last poetry of this period. It's also probably my favourite, as it points to a new landscape of feeling.

# PROEM

## Letters to Khaled Hakim

Dear Khaled Hakim

I knew you 16 going 28 yers ago wen y/ wer pretending to be human

& now Im flying bak – a meat seeking epistel burning in the decayed aire – th spaceshop Old Hill Takaway traveling to its own past for a Chiken Madras & a keema nan –

who wil i meet on th counter, is it me or is it yu –

Are yu stil waiting otside biding yr tyme to smack my uncl in the face? Go eezy on him – we hav oure hole lyf to be a failyur.

I hav vital news. Yu must publish bifor y/ get frozen sholder. In th futur we ar impregnated by Saurian nanobots spred by perfum sampls in wimens magazins. We wer on th brink of getting wiped owt. And it is yorr unborn children who turnd th tyde. I wont tell yu who the mother is in case it afects th futur. But mak sur y/ apply for Child Tax Credits.

No not reely.

How ar yoo?

Ye kno I walkt from it all.

Fifteen yrs ago God dyed to wake me up. I blew my hed owt.

Ive been to th further littoral of realizacion. The Hero w/out a book. I waz *ashik*. I waz rubarb crumbled. I wont tel yoo who dyed – it mite affect yr futur.

I was a pig farmer on th Norfok Brords wen a lone emissary cam stryding acros th growse feels & askd me to riturn:

I cant return, I dont rede anymor.

And he sez, A R Orage sez abot Cyril Connolys 100 Best Books: Wat is anywon doing reeding a hundred books? As if ther ar a hunderd books worth reeding. 10 books are enoufh if you ar *really* to rede. *Won* book – if it is th rite book.

Ah but A R Orage hadnt herd of th badlands razed w/ theorie

the anti essensialist, th alyrick absenteezm, th qweer demanding departments

Oh dont get me started.

Ive got a favor to ask Khaled, Im having cashflow problems & i just need to borrer yr credit cards. Im not even going to tak owt any money, y/ no me. Im doing an event on Satdy, Ile put it strait bk. I no yve got the money ya cheep mendicant dormows. Id reely apreceate this.

I cant even remember, wat did we do in th dark ages?

Can y/ remind me wy I was ever interestid in minimalist poetiks. Th religius feeling has fallen away & only wats left is left.

Yr bro Khaled
*London 2018*

Dere KH

Is it realy yoo. Do yu recognize me – Ive com flashing from
th past in th photon shop at one farthing a second.

And here y/ are the incompetant back of howse,
the next big sandwich,
a linen suted world muzician
th peripatetick howse sitter

Fuk me, you havnt changed.

Work fals down th gradiant at minimum wage
the tyme expanding to fill all posible went
mor seconds more happy happy

Go, yoo hav erned yor varicos vains,
spend it on stilts

How ar y/ going to rescu me in posteritie – are we all being
retraned on permanent Yooth Traning Sceemes ware in th
futur everywon wil hav a job for 15 minits.

I stand w/ sublime tears on the campus tuchline watching th
first XI – my toilet paper is calld Freedom

35 yers ago I was a rickshaw driver in Bangladesh & they
kidnappd me & dressd me up as a New Romantik child
bride; then they put me in a matter transformer w/ Prince &
created a lyf size famin victim in winkelpickers – a moment
reprezenting a constituensy of damige & transgreshion &
other peer consensus. Ther wer peple dying of a plage of
thrush in alternativ kitsch capitals –

But I digress

now i surfice to British post avants – heeres Tim & Jeff
hilson & Karleen & Peter yaeger & Keston & – all wite
collar criminals.

Now I am middel aged & familied & inevitably unemployd
& asking: Who ar the lions of Universiti poetry;

a categorie as definabl as pub rock

luxuriantly varied, somhow divergent practises produse a
monocultur of poets.

Surly ther was a tyme wen inovative poetiks was not tenured
to a Theorhoea that betrays the anxietie of subject status – in
a langwige of hieratick snake oil hucksters

Jezus Crist, do ye kno wat its lyk to be looking at an
online poetiks publisher wich reproduses its contributers
departments & academik status – Senior Lecturer Universiti
this, & Universitie Hed of Creativ that – w/ all th pomp of a
roll call of titled Patrons to an investment bank

Yee myriad few to 'disrupt th workings of capital' & safegard
the power & privalige of akademick robber barons

Let me duble think myself out of that line in cas anywon
ever offers me a job.

Bring me my citasion
bring me my homspun
enter th munisipal gardens of retarded parkys

Now I am old & familyd & inevitably unemployabel, &
asking, Why havent I killd anywon yet? It wd be a releef.
As it wd be a releef to be a human beeng. We can stop
thrashing th wyf & affirm th Logos.

Yoo remind me of my gums exploding lik a fossilizd guppy.

Dere KH, yoo wer a minimalist? I hav no idea. Was yr silens part of a project?

Im sorry mate, id realy lik to help y/ but my moneys al tyed up at th moment Ive got to do a moove & hire a van. Unless I uze the shop for th moov. Wy dont yoo work for my uncel – hes going to be short of a waiyter isnt he?

I name this ship Old Hil Indian Takaway & Van Rentals may God bless her & all who peel the oniuns.

Kindest
Khaled
*Birmingham 1993 or posibly 1998 or 2000-and-somthing*

Dear Khaled

Wy ar yoo leving. I set th controls to 2000-and-sumthing & found thers nowon in.

Actully I dont fancy going back ther.

You kno yu remind me of mee wen I was yorr age –
a subjectspeking Juvenal
an I that dremes of margareen
20 yeres a colapsed khimera w/ th mirrer gazing at me as a
woman

Let me tell y/ abot my vow of silens w/ the Iluminati – it waz after won of my conserts & a woman & her adolesent dawhter gave me a mysterius glossy brochur w/ a card inviting me to join. I think she was waving th 12 yr old girl

as an inishiacion sweetener, but only later did i discover
th girl was the secret Grand – forget abot th girl if i tell y/
abowt her yr life is in danger

But I digress.

So i had to hav sex w/ an oven glov stuffd w/ humus in front
of the asembled lodge & another candidat had to eet th
contents. It cd have bin worse – Robert Mugabe had to fuck
a snowman.

They filmd th ceremony & told us to keep saying th mantras
& wed hear about our aplicasion in due corse. But i now
think its in the LUX collecsion as a Kurt Kren film.

I told y/ not to get me on contempery poetiks. Wat do y/
expect. Generacions of poets riting the picturless langwige &
its refuzals –

a moment wen rockstars rite abot their hotel rooms

Just to be clere, Im onlie uzing th card for lik a minit – I can
put cash in on th Monday.

Y/ no, yoo shd meet th wif. Shell never even kno. I shdnt tell
y/ this but y/ no how ye fantasiz abowt sumone els when ye
mak lov to th wyf – well unfortunatly shes so good looking
I hav fantasiz abot her when Im doing the liv-in nanny. Just
dont think abot her stabbing yoo in th hed w/ a broken
bottle.

Wat do yu say?

Im not even uzing th card – Im just uzing it to get a lone.

I dont kno how i got lyk this. I cant remember anything thees dayz. I dont kno if it was modernizm or th hors tranqwellizers.

Ive got this lik phantom nitemare – acturly I dont no whose dreming. Therz this gostlie figur of a wizend old ladyboy who wud shuffel into his bedroom & hed be woken by her scaley hand under his bedcloze pulling down his pyjamas & slowly fiddling w/ his limp peenis. It was abuse. I thoht I blotted it owt.

But now Im sleepwalking into the spaseship Old Hill & going upstars to th room – & I wake up to find yoo frozen in bed wile what I remember as the old crone is actuully *me* masterbating myself in lonly solase.

Help me bro. You owe me that.

Your
Khaled
*London 2018 and 2000-somthing*

Dere KH

Yore wondering wy we are so pervers – & its a sad nay shocking storie, wan that maks me shudder even now – & ile tell y/ – but onlie yoo.

Won nite I was standing in front of th mirrer in my room, th door opens & in wawks owr grandmother. She closzd th door behind her & coms up to me – & I was frozen. She had her fals teeth in so she didnt look qwite th gargoyel. & she ses to me *Dont say a word – take off my nihtie.*

& terror took hold of me – I cdnt speke I cudnt move. & she sez, *Boy, take off my nihty!*

& somhow I fownd myself reeching to tak off first won sholder & then the other of this Victorian-era nihtgown, & it slipt to the flor.

And she sed *Okay boy, now take off my bra.* & revulsion shook me. It was abuse, I can say it now. I thowht I was going to faynt, but she took hold of my hands & puts them on th bra & seys *My bra! Take it off!*

& I dont even remember how it happend but next thing she was seying, *My pantys boy, my pantys, tak them off, tak them off!*

And and I faynted I must hav faynted bicauz I woke up w/ her on top of me. & i waz nakid. & she slaps me acros th face & she seys – *& dont wear them agen yoo litle gaylord!*

I dont no how I fownd th corage to tell yu all this – how I dowt my own memorie – coz I always confuze her w/ Marlon Brando.

Nah, not reely.

Yore on yr own mate. Wats th matter w/ you, thats owr grandmother, yoo must be sick to beleve that.

Id reely lik to help you bruv. I mene I no weve got a connexion, but I cant tuch my savings. Maybe in a few months wen ive sorted myself out.

Im going yor place rite now. Sume unfinishd biznes w/ sumwon. An it aint ouer uncle.

Take care & send me a pictur of th wyf.

Khaled
*Birmingham 1980-somthing to 2018*

Dear Khaled

I hav terribil news. Yr lif is in danger. No reely. Yu cant cume here.

Dont worry abot the money I got a windfall im fine. After the 3rd baby or 2nd baby I forget wich, I snappt into acsion! – I was put on a barista corse. But they trackd me down & in a hotel lobby I was told I had to go bak to kill you as they culdnt keep up w/ the Child Benefit payments. They sd theyre gonna pore battery acid down his rectum thatll teech me to be a homo. I got four thozand quid to do the job thow! Dont ask abot th wyfe. If i tell you ile have to kill y/ – then shell hav to kill me or ile have to kill her – I forget wich.

Do y/ see John Wilkinson at all – it all began w/ him. Can y/ do me a favor – if I send you a letter can y/ get it to him. I think hes stil in 1986.

Good bye Im relying on yoo to look after yrself mate.

Khaled
*London 2018*

Dere KH

Im sorry to rite but Im going mental. Som fucker clered owt my bank accont & the bank is saying its my signiture.

I kno who it is the gobbling paedo. Im waiting for him owtside of prizon. Im going to melt down yr biology into a metal flavored yogurt & shoot it up yr sinuses – lets see yoo vote in the local elecions coverd in gunk. Ile stick my finger in yr eyebal & the other one in th Nacional Grid.

Brother, ware are yoo?

Ile lerne that crypto diabetik to wast my Tax Contribusians, Im coming rond – no! – Im waiting in my car owtside his street & nock on his door, hes gonna pretend I havent com to tak a shit in his mouth – bang! Ile fuking gaffer tape his hed to his balls. Tho I giv him credit for the poynting on th front of his haus; ye can see how th raiyn has gutterd down th top & softned th bottom if thats subsydens – you can hardly see the fisshure into Hell,

But I digress. Nice bit of work that.

Its lik he got 3 chimpanzees & injected them w/ experimental drugs that sparkt catastrofic growth in th ganglia & frontal lobes, th cranium needing sheering off, wile at th same tym a mad sientist is working on a pocion that grows opozable thumms – till the fuking ape aproches a super bilder who turns up in th morning to finish th job bifore acselerating apoptosis creates footbal sized tumers & it reches the evolucionary stage of taking 3 jobs at onse & onlie turning up wen the plasters wet on the other jobs

But I digres.

How th fuk did they forge my name.

Im sorry I had to get in tuche. I need yr help man. Can y/ giv me th deposit to moove into my flat. I wont even tuche it. Yoo

can just giv it strait to th landlord. How much can y/ spar. Its
not fare mate. Yore use to being a mooch cancer. Im yung.
Can y/ meet me in Brum or ile come to yoo. Are they stil after
me?

Pleeze mate Im dying here.

Khaled
*Birmingham 1994*


Dear Khaleds

Blessings on you both from the Odd Fellows Fraternity of
Bangkok.

For obvious reasons I have been interested in your welfare. In
view of the danger you are in I have chosen a drastic course
– rather like a surgeon who cuts off his limbs – and emptied
both your bank accounts. Have no doubt the money will be
put to philanthropic use by the Mission. We will be building
a jacuzzi for the desperate sex workers and other displaced
teenagers at our Bangkok Lodge.

O brothers, don't follow me out here, the future is worse than
you imagined. The freaknods of academia have won out –
and the planet is policed by Judith Butler fanboys. We have
had our Kristallnacht when thousands of cisgendered Ikea
furnishings were smashed by the Rainbow Coalition. I am
hiding in plain sight as a shilling Jew teaching Transgender
Monkey Studies.

This is your purpose – to cloak me in your cack-coloured
pupae, till you fall away like scabs.

My children, I would not see you serve as the prole meat, the mulch of this Utopia, the fulfillment of Reptilians of the Iluminati. Therefore I have put a contract out on you both to put us all out of our misery. So have the lizards.

Would you do me a favour before you die? Could you find a publisher for some poems I am enclosing? I suggest you give it to Shearsman – they wouldn't know shit from Shelly.

Peace and togetherness from all here.

Amen

Ven. Dr Khaled Hakim KCB, OM, NVQ

*Bangkok 2038*

# Letters from the Takeaway

# Letter to Brakhage

Prelude:

Im flying from you, beloved, Wesleyan & General Insurance, Wele never look into yr windows again. Yr fronts wer wite Victorian gothick, & wen th bus swung rownd, ye cd see riht thru: green w/ fluresent, the moment sculptur holowd thru to the other siyd.

Yr wings an afterthawt. Th sister bilding bridging is alredy rubbl. Im sory. That is th lapidary.

Theyr al winking at me – I no its not transpersonal, but they wer al winking at me – as we swoond in over N.Jersey & the laidowt plots; we ar a golden bal in ech flashing carlot, al the pudels layd owt on th carplants, a flaer trace runing acros windscreens water, sundown wings shadow

the livery is stylish, & y/ dont hav to tip – I wanna be thoz doormen

down St Marks referants qwartermile cleendowt books, boosted castofs, t-shirts piling the nite sidewak ackretiv genre: How to rite in imitaciun when ther isnt a girl i wdnt

Helo Mr Brakhage[1] … umm i cam al th way from England just to say…

---

[1] Note: I plais this pm directly in the auditorium of th Public Theater on Lafayat, & speek to you the urj to butonhol in the shabiest genre of selfserving Leters to Muther: a frend John Wilkinson sd tharee no longer rote w/ the thowht of bein publisht – az i abdicate from al conserns riting wel, in the urj to publish. So long ago. Wy am I riting. I riting in the teeth of sucsess – coming to tel the patriarkal story, that recurent serch for the origin of truth, the word, the law, power

Helo – [2]

I just wanted to say, abowt th theem of *Anticipation of the Niht,* I dont kno how it indicaits or suports wat yu cal the "flaw" of the ending: but i recognizd the jurney into endles niht, the shadow in dorway, & the endles angel of treevains runing away, th wild lihts of the niht –

it lookt liyk a rode moovie to me, i recognizd the fliht in th windscreen thru the niht,

al the kids, wen wed tek off, ther waz a part of disgust, bur I wanted to go cauz to be alive – som goo becauz of misanthropy, but th kids i kno, go to liv

al thoz peple ye kno on th rode, hoo lookt arownd & find frends owtgrown – therither stopt, or theyr ded:

you shd kno, at the end of the escayp, from the family, the hows, the children that wer yoo, ye shd know at the end of th rode is deth.

I recognizd theez emblems, wich belong to us children, that bleeding sky fleeing branches, th faerylites merygorownd wich belong to th Super 8 vizion, even the opositiun of warm & cool & the 2 colors wch belong to dusk, altho i mihtve red that

---

[2] Hello Miles, heers this pece ive been mening to let yoo see for ages. Actualy i came all the way from England to work for my Uncles on 6th St. I used to steal off from the stor for an howr or 2 to catch the Anthologie Arkivz program that was on & i was alwayz late, & the stuckup Festival atendant got iritated – Im working 11 till 11 in the evening humping onion sacks on delivery & this Film Scool degenerat w/ too much qwality lezure time to waste on the surplus valew of avantgard commodity vizions is tellin me off – innat fuckin typical.

experiencing gras in a new visiun, runing, to a new sensorium, of al the ackrecions

but yu shd kno, that yu canot liv in that feeling, running faster & faster than freshnes, becuz ther is deth in that experians.

*Cliche No 1.* Liv evry second lyk its yr last – onlie now i recogniz rejecting al sentimentality for the sentimentality of tales of anomie, looking for deth in lif

ye shd kno yre inviting us to the rihtyous cliche –

Then Mr Brakage askd for qwestions, but yoo had gon alredy

thinking New York had beeten yu – "agen" – wandering thru N.Y. sleeping in alnite moviehouzes, the 23 yr old Brakage apparently thowt after th film he wd kil himself

its so encoraging, the grand old dinosaur of modernism, is as lonly

Imagin that lonlines

at that junctur the trase of th trans poem seeking intuitivly its violent ends, poynting to the structural film, wher in the race to conqer space eny step is a step in th riht direcsion – its that wich maks the masterpece, & consequentlie anackronism

the pickax that wd unfreez th seez

I must hav ast summat abowt narativ, just to tawk to yoo – the
Steinian endlis begining, or returning, a static rythum, but
ther waz a narativ laps puling toward niht, almost a realtim, (I
think i foolishly sd "real tym") & he went of on a tack abowt
verticle narativ wich i realiz was probably a stock spiel [3]

an oedipal pleazur, to denude, to no, to lern the origin & the
end, that evry unvaling of the truth is a staging of the absent
hiden father, the narativ forms of family structurs.

*Cliche No 2.* Somwon askd had yoo taken drugs – & yu sd
Wel wile Iv always beleevd anywon has th riht to do watever
they want w/ thr body – provided it dosnt harm anywon...

The idea any actiun in th world dosnt riple owt into the
univers from the original Leibnitz plop, a curent selfconsiusnes
of awtonomy. Extrordinary partialsihtednes in th hafbakd
eestern ethos

yoo shd kno ther is no posibility of the most destitut absenting
from th world w/owt som trase tuching, even as yr parents left
ther trawma, even az our father left us w/ owers, in ways im
stil finding owt abowt

inherited silens

but failur is not enow to kil yrself

---

[3] 1st Joke, 2nd Shirt: Wen i saw yoo at MOMA (i think) the 8mm
Songs, & yu did exactly th same introductory jok abowt the hipflask
yu cary arownd & uze as a spitoon – it seems to be yor icebraker. I saw
a program poster w/ yu in Milenium – it waz 1972 & yoo wer even
waering th same shirt

but then im not sympathetick to the banalitiz of suicyd

Wen he was 8 he cam home to find his fatherad hangd himself in a radio sopopera – "Arkitect Runover in Fog", th disgizing flesh gon – Al thez crowding providensiz, wat shud i do withem

I cant get bak to th poem, wy isnt it recuring lyk Stein – i dont get it. & yet this presentacion i do extemporary to a program of yr works, the pasagez from *Metafors* hafpat, I memoriz, & they becom my poetri – [4]

Iv spoken befor to peepl, reding *Antisipacions* violent swishpans & focus flatening spais, & i new exactly wat it lookt lyk. Wat i waznt prepard for, peple wawking owt the hyperventilats in my film, & i just wanted to say, all the damijd children of my auditorium – it waz my film

.................................................................................

---

[4] Imagin an I unruld by manmaid perspectiv, an I that dos not respond to th name of enything but must encownter eche object. How many colurs in a feild to the crawling baby unaware of 'Green'...By spiting on th lens yecan thwart focal intent. By handholding th camera ye can inherit worlds of space...

Thoz ears are fingers & the noz a nuckle impeding the liht...Ye can uze the filters of th world, fog, downpor, unbalansd lihts, thoz taboo hrs the labs wil garantee nothing

Wen i introdusd myself inicialy I thowt it waz to her in th film; but then at Segue i herd "he has al theez wimen & they al look lyk Jane." Im sory to say i herd yoo referd to as a Gote. Perhaps theyr all blond & al cald Jane. But she waz very nise to me & understood i wanted to tawk to yu. I cam al the way from England to tawk to yu, yoo wer very nice to me: turnd owt the sad trans figur

an analog for the delicat riter, for a duble, another body my projecsion enacted

pure unideological existenshial reeder who 'freely' perseves & lerns from eche confrontasion w/ th page [5]


that he waz az lonly, as it is wonderful yoo ar as lonly, but in futur I am a ded underated master & ther is no help; how can we conect the act of creating, just then, wen i am a failyer & alon, just now, wen yoo ar so alone

Heer it is. The wds did not spring to cal. Heer is another publick transport, trasing the trans to Astor Plais

Meditait on failur. I dont kno wat it is, looking in a namless stainles steel alien twinservis kiosk w/ crome shutters down: look in, the observer carris a blak vail

---

[5] In hiz powerful fenomenology a curious tension – the riting not riting of film. Narrativ gleend thru vizions diferenciasion in spase, between the parts of a sentens, az wel as plezures temporal deferment, becuz a sentense canot be red at wonce. Vizion dispensing immediate punctual plenitude of conshiusnes – visions mening reveeld in a flash of presens, repeeted in relacional iteratiun, meening met again & again to displase & defer that epiphany

I waz doing it liyk a poet. Peple must think im loony. I was doing it lik failur.

Sentimental 'meaning' rears in a last cliche of New York, significans of th moment, to go home. How many tyms we hav don this. Lingering on the niht arownd as fishei niyht

I herd the buskers on th platform. Th poepl ringd rownd 12 o clok. I stept by & throw change, & lookt too, cauz they wer too good for th subway & lookt traind, th dublebais her violin stroks taps so tiht, she lookt at yu lyk she cd be looking at yoo, even the gitarist w/his fine fowk voyce & thr balad that sang Wd he sleep in her bed agen; [6]

Train com roring owt, ye saw in th flashing of frames the shadowplay, stil evrything is serius

*N train to Astoria – Watch the doors –*

Thees 3 they belong to me – holding won end of the carige, & me – dazed Columbian Bangladeshi midnite travelers hoo hav not put in thr qwarter clap in tym

ther is a superiority in this pozition, ther is that melting contact lens in the I agen, & i am in another train, god applawds w/ things on hiz mind, mimicking human behaviur hiz own sufering

---

[6] I lookt for yoo in the Sentral Libry musick shelvs in Birmingham. The refrain of The Somthings Dawter together w/ N train to Astoria – Watch the doors recurs thru the rest of th poem

Ile have it again


that line & yelow train of windows abov that lyn of mooving
car liyts in the black bridge girders – I never saw that, I never
ever saw that.


If theyd let me i wd liv in Grand Sentral St, but wen he red
Conjuncsions sat in the verge of the Interstait crickets, it waz
th first tim hed felt gras in 2 months.

......................................................................................


The sentiment wich runs thru the subway sene, is a dreary
social realism Labor MP passd over for Cabinet Ofis & failing
marige; watching stripers w/ seetlods of flatcaps, somwons
sqweezing the hips of th blond on th bar as hez geting pist in
town, looking at the ads for French models

When yu pass the Italians, w/ th fase lyk Holy Smoke
remember yre a free animal


Alredy its fawling – O darlings – I havnt had summer


I am alredy sick. I am alredy sick. I am alredy sick. I am alredy
sick.

......................................................................................

*Cliche No 3. The Outsider:* Im not suseptable to certen modes of alienashion – wile marveling the perfecksion of Camus, I thowt, Wat a spineles maggot, im shur not the respons he intended. To thos protagonists of a vage lack i hav an empirickal positivist urge to say Pul yrself together yoo utter shower.

Th poynt of th poem is som shit lyk th song is too gud & th girl too pritee – it hurts, the nite is so beutiful it hurts

Th poynt is I shud be able to say it, Im a failyer – Oh no Im bak in New York [7]

The rest of th poem was spent w/ th line of *I am a failyer.*

............................................................

The struktur in th poem is the adress to somwon famus

The reson for this is I just dont caer anymor

---

[7] Oh no Im back in England – & im still a failur. & still i havent savd the Wesleyan & General Insurans bldg. & failyur defeets riting.

*Postscript:*

Pleez help me Mr Brakage, just now, wen I am so secur &
distracted, as i com to tel the patriarkal story

I cant get back to th poem, another time at riht angels to real
tym – having a good tyme in illuzionist spayce, from social
spaic, from this real, into a difrant rezidens fantasiez snikering
fantazms

persistans of beleef in the Letter az a real letter owt ther, in
simultaneous existans w/ identificasion structurs, this Letter as
profeshional literatur, iluzionist practise w/ an arkitectonicks
uneffast

disalow projecsion into that tym as real, into this space

redirect the reder to the wooden handle of a rememberd
umbrela, this page as imagind by flames, & the flesh of the I
reding this –

The opacity of th riting iz the dificultiez of wat is actual the
engagement w/ th conkrete, words az sensa

rezist the liht, reflect it, to block off owr seeing THRU INTO
I imagin th letter yu wd rite, braking & losing syntax in the
pedantick osiosities, th stunning emphases on prepozicions,
& the insistans on the most banal re-vizions of words; slowing
th site of reding, geting to particluar numinous

I dunno how you can rite so crapily.

Why am I such a ded neck Mr Brakhage. Why do i not engage eny longer. Why was it necesary to lop off my deluzions to get a life. Why do i prefer decorating th bathroom to coming to senses. Wat has happend to the spiritual abnegacion & grant endowment cynicizm. Do yu still SEE THRU INTO. Im finding life as a modernist asetick depresing. Heers yu poynting owt external sownds relaciun to inner ear eye & pulse events & i just wanna rip somwons hed off

Dere Mr Brakhage, so litle extasy, teche me to becom liht [8]

---

[8] the horizon lines & bakgrownd shaps batering th form of the horsback rider as the camera moovs w/ it, the curvs of th tunel exploding away from the pursued, camera folowing, & the tunel perspectiv on the pursuer, camera preseeding

eywize, & th very comet of its overhed throw from projector to screen wil intreeg yu so deeply that its fingering play wil move integraly w/ wats reflected, a comettail integrity wich wd leed bak finaly to the film creator.

The time of th poem includs The First New York Internacional Festival of the Arts (Film as Vizion program at the Publick)

The reding includs *The Avantgard Film* Ed. P. Adams Sitney, *The Anti Narrativ* P. Gidal (Screen Summer 1979), *The Plezure of th Text* R. Barthes, *Studio Internacional* Nov/Dec 1975, *The Middle Way Journal of the Buddhist Society* (Spring & Winter 1991)

Birmingham 1989/91

# Letter to Antin

Dear Nicholas

This is part of the poem. I wonder if yd be interested in some of my performativ werk. Ive lately been occupyd w/ episolary forms, wich is an enactment of riting. I realy wanted to giv a long piece, my 2nd Letter to Brakhage. This is a performans poem wch givs y/ an idea of wat i do in performans & episolary.

I wen to the Poetry Library insid the Festival hal. A realy swanky place. & i was dying to go to the toilet first wich is conveniently just outside it on the 5th Level. & inside wer a cuple of ruff trayd who sort of flattend themselvs up against th urinals syde by syde & lookt at me out the corner of thr eye.

& id only gon in to wash up. I thght, Oh its a cotage – I thght it was odd this place in the Festival Hall outsid the Poetry Libry shd be chose to coksuck, & what kynd of clientel they got. & i lyked that. It felt lyk poetry was beeng kept alive. Caus ther wer mor peple in the toilet than the libry.

Its the best stockt plais for new poetry & peeriodicals anywher heer, & id gon in to check up on a poet w/ affinitees – David Antin, & i notisd how morglike it was – somwon was asleep & otherwys it was in profownd

Ive com to be unable realy to rede w/o mowthing. I remember i was trying to rede Rimbaud & lern French, & im speking it to get the hang. After 3 weeks i wen into the Central Libry & took down a book, & i fownd cauz i cdnt actually *say* the words w/out disturbing other peple & them thinking i was thick – i literaly cdnt understand it. Saying translyted the sines. If i tryd doing it sowndles – as weve al lernt – i cdnt reed.

I waz thinking this caus id just been reding Onians abowt the Gk Homeric lokation of the seet of consciusnes or inteligens (phrenes) in the lungs – lyk children think, thauwt is in the mouth.

They cald me Owwa in Bangladesh, becaus i wasnt fluent in Bengali, & not beeng fluent in langwage i had no idiom of ordnary lif. It meens idiot, literaly dumm. They wernt teken in by my books.

This is how peeple red. I was in that Poetry library w/ all its roling stacks wich is ment as absolute repozitory or depozitry, & intrested peopl – profeshnals – com & reserch. I dont kno what for. Its hard me for not to wish i was w/ the tee room boyz in the toylet. I thawt i shd hav gon in & sd *Lissen if yu dont giv me som of yer ars im gonna stick my fist up it.* Im caerful of my fascist impuls to burn appropriat librys.

I recal reding abowt St Ambrose hoo was a wunder to the other monks becauz he cd actualy rede w/o mooving his lips. Do ye kno what the cells thees carrels wer for – it was so they dint disturb other monks wen reding the Bible. Becus nowon was abl to reed silently. Becaus we hav learnt to see nothing. Dont worry if i tawk beneth you – its part of the grater redundancie of orality – y/ can drop in or owt, becuse i dont speke to a supereleet – of one.

I didnt hav to think of this as a poem. The occazion of poetrie is simply a decision. I gus in th toilet theyr disturbd felating. I gos into th libry its unnatural qwiet, becaus thouht is in th mouth. Its not becuz Antin was saying somthing abowt myth muthos is simply saying

Rather the poetic brain begins organizing th flux of my living into connexion. I think in form.

Im looking up a talk poet whos work isnt even a scor, only a record; its only strange it dosnt mak sens mor ofen. Im lookin up a magazene Talus i can giv somthing to, & now ive had the idea i can transpoze this into a Letter to Antin.

Dere Mr Antin, yr poem tawkd me out of my afair. Wed bin having a ruff time anyway & im down ere cauz of it. This publick occazion poem that seems to be looking for principls of agreement in lov, in mariage, & wch pretends to a matur judgemnt, & wch is reely looking for a way out yr prezent afair. Ye can see it in this pat opposition, analogie w/ the story abowt yr erlier affaer wch is so obviusly unsatisfactory, & Eli hoo is so obviusly somthing els – oh yeeah. I dont kno if yu kno it. I usd th poem (found) as a sign, as magik.

Im so misrable Mr Antin – I just watcht the Watson-Eubank fiht & when he yad him down i jumpt up & bangd my hed against the beem i hadnt been so happy all week; & wen the referee stopt the fiyt i hadnt been so unhappy al week. Three seconds later Eubank got up & knokd down Watson. It meks me think thoz Budhist w/ ther distrust of emotion, this paranoyac retreet from activitie into the mandarin contemplativ, maybe they got it rite. If Abbie ad been ther id hav puncht the shit ourof her. In my poems im always the most ridickulus won.

I did a performance last tym wich dint werk becuz i got cawt up w/ yr Sokratic curv of inqwirie insted of keeping to my short agressiv – in, owt. i dont want nufin to do w/ al that sweet reesonablnes saintly seeking after process

Look at this performanse poem – its al bleeding level discours like wat yu do – whers the gimicks the acting i stick in look at thes fuckin paragrafs, im suckt into tropes that arent nemonic

the more i kno abowt yr work the less i wanna no – i shd stick w/ the fiers campiness. Hoo can bor peeple better w/ yr mode same w/ that L=A=N=G=W=I=G=E textualitie guff they starrid afecting me owt of wat i do – what *doo* i do – a lone popular polemick against the cors of poetick use & transmishon sins the Renaisance. Im caerful of my conformist streek.

Wen ise a kid & had suss but i always fownd it dificult to argu my intuicions from werking clas values – becauz langwage & reazon wer the langwij & reson of a class literat; & i had to lern the langwige of categories to lern i didn hav the langwage of categoris

I realiz im being drawn into dogmatizing oral modes, cauz nobody nos wat im doing, so not only do i hate all practicioners of anything that looks lyk vers, i ate everythink that dosnt qwestion why its in a book, the whol fuking inteeriorizd seeking after identity wch is the excuse for poeticks

hyding in som fen for 12 yers then inflicting craftid pietis on us – drop ded git.

I jus thowht Mr Antin yd lyk to kno that yre not qwite an isolated voyce, if not a sad lonelie old man w/out my lov then furrowing a lon trayl up yr arsole. Thers somwon in Birmingam hoo was doing poems w/ a prozody of comutativ verbiag, caus wat the fuck, & I know hoo yoo ar, & heer wer at the interfase of a hole changeover from an irelevant cultur – but nobodie nows it

*Birmingham Oct 1991*

# Run Pm

After i missd th morning, this shd hav been a Hymn to Liyht.

Seeing with Liyt is rare, & springliyt is rarest. My noze flummoxt w/ smel.

So otherwiz it is slugish, go for a run. Owt of a Cup final. & later the Bregenzer festspiel & later

Economick in stryd. Runing w/ incorruptibl joynts, tender. w/ keez & a sayfty pin holding my flys.

& on Church Hil not for th first tym th evry erth in relaciun blu to wite sky, unseen crowding up city.

hevy underfoot park & trot.

Heer acros th fencing, the ruind wiyt ston of th semetary. O yeah, obvius the Muzlim graivs wer busted at th base, just the imigrant slabs. But it al looks nackerd hill.

Trot, war fame sun has not dryd the edges.

Waer is the runing poem going revisited, why is the pm. Ar we pretending to see my lov

*Ya, Kev.* But we must run, for Imelda is again too much, & i too litel… I dont wannu do it anymor. Its broke down

this diction of ezy clipt, thats the form of day to day epifenomenalism – history all is history

I dont understand wy uze thees special modes, watever historical speech patern – the excizion of articls, prepozicion, an overburdening copula – or the overburdening indeterminat preposicions stragling th liyn –

noone qwestions why this, wy poetry. Wy this exacted flux

It doznt mayk sens to me, non of it ansers. Why this –

lapidary of sens.

Tayk th cirkit, & at the park bowndary, go bak

Heer broken acsess to Handsworth semetry, shd be gud for som thowhts. But no notebook so no poem.

& straitway ther snapt crossiz & the fawlen stonz: ah lying in th shalow bed, a carven 3 foot figur, marbel w/ its hed mising – othersiz shd i hav nickt it. Did somwon realy chizel clasical folds liyk thoze reproducsions.

Wawk down the wooded sunlit pyls: but no notbook so no poem. But afeckting inscriptions of Edwardian; & familis under toomstone, but no glases. & leningtoos & vandalizd.

Just one – perhaps a suspicius congregacion over at Church Hill, – a blak broken tablet, grayt falen sheald, & at its shard end held water in basin. & at its hed inscripcion had pited & honeycomd owt in atricion, & also holows, as armadillo osify into holows.

But ther waz only a baer inoquous tree to look up. & heer won fantastick trunk limb that grew over into a whiplash.

So thru, looking for the moslims his unkl, spiting skin went thru & thru th genrel mischif who sez deth is the end of truble.

Run poem revizit the original isnt –

I dont understand wat this dictiun is – to run thru 6 monkeys tapping typriters hoo wil eventualy discover the syntactik relaycions to poetry is, cuz i dont kno

if styl *Sulfur* is expreshion of forms of fals conshiusnes, then synapsiz colapst, veleity working thru syntax

Wy this – wy this

This is th part fr the other siyd of th fens. The magpys, as i wawkt rownd, & up, & bak to th top. Valted the mucus wal, onto th rode. Lets run. Lets run bak (onions). So trot hyding my flyz.

Th lihte is stil so hony it hurts.

O shit! heer this joyus girl, i duckt, on Heethfeild Rd is thumming a lift

That hurts me so. This is th sanctiun to rite this – but not yoo to reed. Ile never stop riting proz.

oh shit oh shit heer is the Breygenzer festspeil: hav i fukd won of th litel stage animals.

& then into Amazon raynforest with hiz dinner. & now a 30 yr old myopick ashole martinet acros Austrailia – having livd his lif bakward – how to find his way bak into th natur of his destiny.

......................................................

# Pound me a Tarentela w/ Jewzharp

*Fuk off —*
*Its th Pity we cant tayk!*
*Its th Pity we cant tayk!*


*Birmingham Oct 1991*

# Second Letter to Brakhage

Dear Mr Brakhage

Ye bastard did it to me agen. I sd its unfair to everywone else to show his film w/ thers.

Im interested in entirely expository; as im interested in criteqes i entirely disrespect: Lukacs for instans, whose reding of modernism in the novel leading to the ahistorical & an impotense of action, that the subject ironicly then becoms the impossibility of writing, is i think valid

Moira cajoald me into coming down for the premiere of *Faust IV* at th London Co-op & a "brelliant" party on Sunday, & my Fufoos in hospital w/a new baby. Allow me to tedium; there is no background singing here, ther is no notion of what im dg except 2nd Letter to Brakhage

becaus the Ox is inadequat cdnt tel me Pikeys address of cours i miss them at Victoria;

Moira is a bastard during screenings but even mor stressdout w/ evry pece of eqwipment for differant formats of the screening bust. So i shant be staying w/Moira & the program (£2.50) is weak im disappointed my revisiting to London is going to be ordinary & frendless. Bere w/this; this is no background, ther is only retracing as far as the epiphany rings ahed extend

Christine had giv me Cosmic Rays no., & he dosent answer, Sassas no. dosnt answer so they must have uppd & relocated wile fufoo is in hospital, Malu has managd to fly off to Chekhoslovakia for a few days opportunistic feeling the typriter of the people Andy says he wont be back til 2 or 3; Id like to hang out & stop w/ Moira; im so broke

So this screening is over, is hardly part of yr pm; anyway i can stay w/ Moira i just have to watch her eet: but unwinding w/a few people abowt the formativ orthodoxies of Le Grice & Gidal & some uninteresting male feminism on the restricted emocional blocks availabl to men she locks up & we goo home w.out eeting.

Her bedroom was frozen. She asks abowt the first film but if i hear one more Voiceover about 'presense' & 'absences' & the Other im going to puke. I am interested the ways in wich artists work w/in fashions of mutualy reinforcing common discors models of marginal peer pressur. I include this because i like to hav bits w/ buzzwords from critikal theory it helps to place it w/ L=A=N=G=W=I=G=E poetics

Moira dosnt sleep for the disasters i thght it was me. We goo in th fresh day to Camden in her spiffy miniskirt outfit to eet but her brother dosnt show at Cafe Delanceys beutiful out-of-work actor waiters

This is relevant becus ive hardly ever recald dreams. A number of men are esier to manipulate; & the last cuple of years strain she just wans to start filming & not be responsibile, thats what she says. I just want to dump this bitch, im looking for the One, i seys.

I had thees dreams waking & dozing thru th morning; in a howshold akin to Moiras on a lake & in the room a girl is so taken w/ me, i dont get when she gos off me completly; owtside ther seems a spy senario in the supermarket i turn to see som nun shooting me w/a single lens form behind her purdah; I snatch th lens & in cloze th police survaillanse but they cant use overt force; i want to know whats going on & as th plaincloz usher me owt to help in enqwiries holding my arms, we are out on th bayside & i gestur first one direcsion then the other all natural lyk so i can get th leverage to hurl the cameralens into the lake. Maybe thel do me over theyr not worrid, out com all the other skindivers a submarene

Moira sugests properly feminin anxietis coming to surface thats so convencional & owt of all the people Ive never bin so secure in ages. I hav to spend a fiver on the meal. This is al relevant or cd be.

Cut cut – the narrativ cement, Mr Brakhage. I dont know wat to do putting it all in, what to do w/owt diaristic instruction, w/ no 'point';

setting events in thr proper order as "universal history" with "no theoretical armature." Im so sorry, ive faild agen, i thght it was somthing els, another performance, but its the same thing, unpicks the literal surface of the literal surface

Mr Brakhage we goo back to the Coop & i try to mek myself useful w/ Greg setting up th video projector & th monitors in th palm court i dont kno the first fuck abowt video teknology.

I gorra tell you, the (film) installation *You Heard What She Sd – Now What Did She Tell You* in the old Music Colective, a cold space curtaind off w/ black cutowts in them for hafadozen projector loops onto a central religius space, three gauzes or crepes hanging from the ceiling to encloze vertical spase, the images of loopd grainy synecdokhic torso hands is just so sensuous; her voice clicking indecipherable endlessly

Can i ly & pretend its not now, can it lie reconstucted if Id lost another notebook after N.York, thisd be fuckt sir, how wd memory fake it again & again, how narrativity is ever lost, but thats not the point, the 'point' was possibly another narrativity or som point

This notebook lying in the editsuete after the Wide Angle party was lockd up; & i got Hossein to pick it up after a wk, this poem placd in my hand; sitting in Hossains w/ thir flu drinking hiself ratfacd the unknon controld by indisputable expression [1]

I shd be owt scoring agen befor Chrismas, shd be dg this shd be dg that, that was almost now

Can i remember it – thats all structure is – cd i perform it –

.................................................................

& now im coming down w/ thr flu....

---

[1] To Hossein:– Shd i be botherin to argu his 19th C idea of "scientifk" I cdnt think of anyone less "scientifick" – this obsession w/ a production so written that production is "mekanical", rather than discovering during the writing

the so calld science in this system as disgised metafor his Western cultural bias (sins Plato) toward a kind of wacko irrational worship of the logocentrick

& now Im not down w/ flu, & its still now


Dear M, you must get me to tell A how he miht have had foisted on him:

this girl came up wher i was perchd on the back benches & was looking for a place to crash: a refugee fr the Danish Film Coop since a week; shed been attackt by a blak taxi driver whod promisd a lift to Bristol – what cd i say – I beleved her. I knew her – she was the kook had put up the 2 pages on the bilbord for accomodation (promising *Blonde – blue eyes!*) in the most warpd handriting.

But i have to beleve her so who can i land her w/, Can she drop her frend. So i ask Moira like she gave the quid to the nice black tramp at the tube; Moira cant but she says, *& im certainly not sharing my bed w/a stranger* wch is a disapointing matter of principle. Sogand is here for her premiere & in th pitch dark the sound fucks up agen – *Palilmpsesta* – the title is like mine

If i refuse indirectness paratactics, is what im dg just return of repressd tale – it hardly seems worth it

So peple, flush thru another notebook, ring Cosmic Ray he cant accomodate, stil meet tomorrow, altho i let Christine go w/out asking her; I finally reach *Sassas*, I go tomorrow. Ive explaind to Anna im working at Wide Angle in Bham so it wd be esier to help (dick) her ther she cd come to the party & eet. When i ask what she will be dg shes going to Portsmouth tomorrow, to the Workshop to borrow 16mm equipment; wch is surprising when she dosnt know wher shes staying fr one day to th next: she seems impressd

Back w/ Anna shes found someone whol help in the interval.

After the interval they hav another crack at Sogands & afterwards she gets me to yell The filmmaker wd like to say the sound was out of synck & shes gon. Anna has second thghts, she dosnt like to trust this person she trusts me. I hope thees addresses ive giv dont return to hawnt me. Do i forgo the party & take her to As.

..................................................................

it was yr film that made it worthwil Mr Brakhage; i dont understand what the emotion was abowt this time Mr Brakhage, i dont understand why my chest constricted it was alriht this tim, why was it saying its all alrit: the Ox is inadequat & a bullshitter; Moira is coming down w/ all this kind of irk about 'fairwether frends' & sick of organizing peoples problems wch is so sorry for itself; this waif as the Israeli seys is "cuckoo" & like the Ox somone abusd now propagating abuse; maybe im imperialistick

numbd speechles ikon maker stumbling on in forward progres w/ consuming revolucionary zeal, one mor unnecessarie convencion after the next as he approche the essence of his single medium – phallocratick masterie needful personal devastaycion as heros & maisterpeces forged in the firey travail of this religyious quest for kultural puritie


what dos it mene yr turning to sownd, I aknowledge its the riht kind of trecherous sound – is ther a template for the atonal sensibility, tambres of isolacion – do yoo sense somthing in th desert th near transcendent zone, you seemd at home

the film was coming *back*, th blobs of red sundown shaking as water in tines of electronik scor, coming owt of black leder – landscapes dionysian refusal to limit scrub clered of human demarcacions

except one pure tarmac, shaking bus window desert genre

eche shivering aspect ratio the (op)position of higher mening lower appearans… only riting emerges as an endless horizontal pressur that disolvs boundaris… hart & breth it was coming on; how can i speke in such repressd prosody, when the subject is such song – is ther a mesure


Dear Mr Brakhage, it was all rite to be owt of it, i lened across th Waif & sd to Moira Its unfair to others to show his work after. Teknical masterie, intuited exactness, yr irrelevance now. Thinking on it, it isnt as wild as *Anticipation* [2]
But it still isnt reson for writing

---

[2] I forgot to tell you I herd the musick in Anticipation, recapitulacions variation, if i counted the frames wd it disclose kabbalistick structur, a spiritual teknick of the hyperventilat

So this screening is over, is hardly part of yr poem; people wd com up, David Rimmer, & compliment me on Sogands film – I toldem Sogand helpd me a lot – I shdve been showing a film.

Anna has found somone whol help… she has second thghts,

Moira seems left to arrange taxis to the end-of-Festival party & then people just disappear so its not 2 taxis its one, then its a palavar whos using th taxi me & th waif & Slim – caus one of Moiras handmaidens says hed rather go home & maybe make his own way – & Moiras upset caus this taxis rather for somone like him. Alredy i look toward the end wher intension casts directly back across one long copula, & then as we gerowt Moira says *Whos paying for that woman – who dos she think she is,*

Anna looks at the do in the NFT foyerful festival administators & seys *This is joke* corporat mania for temperance clarity individual identiti clere distinction of forms Chinese food & drink, & other centralizd planning; thers nothing to say heer, triteness dissipating, Anna finds the Israeli whol put her up, tracts of connectiv

I do speke to one girl who again, was affected by the Brakhage, always "so emotional"; how do others recongnize this emotion

David Rimmer & Moira ar baiting ech others subsidy: *As one of the few survivors from th first London screening of Art of Vision in 1967* I forget what were talking… the empiricist-optical-formal-pure experiens fr the impure jabber of talk – thes kultural temples bilt w/ the surplus of ingenius instrumentalists

Moira is looking for her brakdown after th festival we leve her across into the pavilion big band playing La Bamba spooning w/ som Christian th longlimbd hoyden doing th pony in the rosy tentlight


Dear Slim, i didnt kno who you was i was pushd w/ by Moira in the alcove, yu nearly lost my bag, yoo wer the kid did the Equus film th first niht w/the garbled sound coming underwater I thght it was deliberat I likd it – it was the best (funiest), except for the opening closeshot of the running legs on th moor in comparison w/the rest of this qwirky film offended my modernist stylizing (of) reality: the idea as i sd that ther is an unmediated reality that y/can transparently re-present is suspicius he agreed: imagin this, long shot of figur belting along dunes, closeshot backtracking on scarpy dips, the runner trying to run slow enow for camera to keep up. But you wd have likt it Mr Brakhage, probably becus th shortwave sownd was indecipherable. Do you think i shd rite a piece on humour in yr films Mr Brakhage


...........................................................


I am unclene in the *Shabebarat,* the angels do not come to me but the mening is, it is now *Shabebarat* – where is mening w/ an attension span of 2 weeks – Ive been reading the Blu Book but stil no meaning, what is written scrubd clean of feeling... meere absorption of art into histori


the Israeli dosnt know whats happening, *Sure if she wants a place to stay no problem, But,* he points to his hed, *Shes cuckoo.* Sins she aproached me i supose shes been hitting peple every hafhour – but they ar all men. Thers nothing mor of Moiras brakdown passage; her Handmaiden reenters the pm;

loneliness of the dance;

til shes deserted, til she drags me, til she wants to spoon w/ me
& I am convincd it is *not* a good idea, till somthing, i thght
it was Christian going off w/ this girl of his, tips her over
her brakedown stupor; & me & slim Steven & Handmaiden
tek turns keeping her keeling over, mostly me in the end of
festival party – thers the doorman shed brushd aside for his
officiousnes as wed com in, & I seem to be holding the only
paralytik in th ball. I dont remember but im not impresst w/
this – all that assurans in the tale – its just bullshit.

Dear Moira – they are so pacient i am unimpresst I was invited
down & its inconsiderat we cdnt find her addres in her bag
shes so drunk – i dont kno wher she livs. Steven put us up (6
quid) thoh the driver is extreemely unsure about any woman
throwing up in his car. I dont remember, unfolding her in
th freezing maybe dilapidated, we lay Moira down in the
bedroom he says *Its quite all rite let her be sick* hes so pacient,
with no liht, nomadic caus the walls are furs or therare furs
on the bed. Me & Slim play chess till 5. Ar you interested in
chess. It is so fucking freezing Slim wonders wat becom of the
Waif – he had offerd

Dear Moira, its not even yr pm, in the morning i haf to retell
y/ the events then retel, – Was she embarrasing, – What was
she dg w/ Christian – were lying ther & its stil tedius: *Yd got
like – a typical Irish incoherent* – she turnd away, Oh she ses
Im not listning anymore to this racist – it makes me so angry
when i hear the Irish stereotypd as drunken

shel never let me hear the last, Ile never be a Houseboy: she
says *Yre riht, you probably are turning strait…tel me everything,
I have to know this!* I wdnt like to be around if she was a
Chinese communist. I find out she did exactly the same at
last yers ball.

So we kiss her in the kitchen shes going to David Rimmer, mind you my breth stank, she sd *What do you mene "flippd" – did I embarras Christian* – I sd he probably thght you wer having some menopausal freak, wch she took as sexist, wch was a mistake fucking Irish bint; but it was unthinking, so more damning, but *I* didnt say that – *hee* thoght it.

Dear Slim, im sorry you figur so litle in the night, thers nothing of the performance in St Martins window Nietzches eternal resons spider, I dont remember wat it was – In the pm, you were supposd to help rite it [3]

the possibility that we do 'mene' that wichas had its meaning canceld by us… what to do 'in' the nothing left by hiatus – thoh sceptical how i "drain" the poetick out, or ptry out of ptry

What i forget becoms structural, working fr ruptur to ruptur – You sd *Yve got to reconfuse the center.*

I forgd a new 1 day pass but we must warn you Mr Brakhage they dont go thru the ticket barriers: he sd *Do you mind if i dont leve w/ you – im feeling qwite strange i need to be by myself for a wile – its a nice feeling*

As quikly as posible – acros this passage. I gooz to *Fufoos* where shes stil in hospital & thers just th kids I get fed & in the erly evening i go over w/ Haroon to Whitechapel Hosp. & i can only afford the 2 pound flowers. *Fufoo* has blood pressur, the baby is hairy, the student nurs is nice, the Sister is a baboon

---

[3] Tell Jo Pryde, In performance y/ confront the simplist quest of post-modernism – Like me. This is the interesting bit: forget evrything els. Is every fuckin formalism in guize a strategy to be a sociopath, these consiously sustaynd poverties of langwage, the dificulties in revenge

& *fufoo* nods & grins lyk an idiot when shes scolded, & after the curtain isn allowd drawn fr visitors I have words

So i leve at 8 & ring Cosmic Ray not to make too much as ive eeten & get details to his place – as quick as posible – hes making the leek stew & we catch up Oh you gorra read the letter fr his boss: *For some time now we have been unhappy w/ the level of committment you hav shown – we are a growing organization of dynamick landscap gardening, & we cannot find place for the aethereal muzings of a poet.* His Senegaleze storie was a much wilder film tryin to make it thru Africkan buroacracy than his film & i stuff my face w/ leekstew

We go to bed after midnite, & then som womans voyce coms thru the letterbox *Raay, oh Raaay*, I thght it was for me, asking to let her in; but Ray, i never told you, but somtime in th night i catch my dreme trickling hot urine & i suddenly realize & wake to my uncontrold hose tha is weeing on my thighs as i lie on my side,

Mr Brakhage roll up experiense what doz it mean

I dont kno – sometims i wake my groyne sticky w/ swet – but i wait if the bath temperacure of th weed sheets is going to freeze into somthing horrible like i remember fr childhood, & it freezed into somthing wet & horible I cant beleve

I remember i thght how my anguish allayd as it dryd evaporating on my body becus i dont remember the angwish – the long niht hugging this piss, undeserving, as ever to to recenter confusion

I wanted to tel you Ray, i wanted to throw my ridiculusness on yr gd humour; I was going to tel him id spunkt up in the niht & washd it whil he was out; but as my bodyheat evaporated thru th nite, so th shame slipt. I wonder if Ray wil still talk to me when he finds owt i piddled next to him; aah evrybody probably wees in it, he probably wees in it himself.

Dear Mr Brakhage, what dos it mene, do you suffer fr this problem; it has a long history in Romanticizm i imagin. Even Moira, she was much mor likly to urinate in her sleep, even shee didnt. Was Moira riht. Did I wee in my sleep fr her sugestion.

What dreary epifhany – rites the pre-text –

& suddenly the whole narrativ trajectory is apparent, & working in a fluidity, untidy verbal equasions trying (not) to say somthing, wch avoids the anxiety of knowing, bump utter bathos – an emptying of meaning & a further displacement of self ... that denial or mocking of the abstract that lust for the represented – what does the totally discursiv look lik – the forms of affability, will anyone still be frends

Slim bringing St Martins weariness of St Martins, Moiras *Can she wear a miniskirt after her period, What els did she do at the Party.* As a British Counsil representativ of experimental film, do you think that right sir. I describe her untypically as i kno she has coresponded w/ you, tho ther is som aspect of yr filmmaking apparently "patriarkal" I shd poynt out that i reckon she wants to get off w/ you. The only one who seems fully helthy is Ray in his dynamick landscayp of ethereal musings [4]

Dear Cosmic Ray, you wanted to kno What were you *up* to last nite – some secret rite:

after y/ left for work Ray i tippytoed into the bathroom to wash this dryd piss on me, but the sheet was stil widely staind, th bed smelld & damp, I had to drape it over yr arkhaic convector heter, & then i turnd the matress over – if you check Ray, th mattress has been turnd & so has th sheet; i talkd w/ that wild woman waiting for them to dry & left for Victoria in the afternoon, & tell Enda i took 25 pence or so fr his change but i was so broke O god it sounds wors than it is!

yre asking like i know what im dg – everything is transparently somthing els – the reduced menings of minimalism... narrativ like a bad striptese discover weve reched bone & there is nothing left;

---

[4] The Waif was last herd of, closing out ironies, in Picadilly Circus midnite "in a bad way", wher the Ox found hisself a job at the big allniht record shop ther, if it isnt bullshit.

& Grandaunt Tiger cryed out & died. The flatness of th telling catches the authentick nurserie tone: the lack of affect of the premoral child

the 'publick' as opposd to the actual audience wch exerts pressur... visible in paws intonacion outburst nonsequitor all the inflexions of real speech another excuse to be a derelict – noone takes me seriusly as it is

So whar is it all abowt – can ther be a moral about overeeting... a tiht mode w/ little room in form or content a strong intensional grip on the image: now to underlin state of mind & put it beyond negociation depresion – wher the 'fixt' picture wil inflikt its hopelesnes – & the tru fear rise, that its a lode of crap

convencians of nonrepresentational abrupt brushmarks

ending in deferment to authoritie

The reding covers *The Blue Book* (Witgenstein) *Langwage & Mind* (Chomsky) *Identity A Pm* (Stein) *Critical Inquiry* (Winter 1989. Robert Morris et al) *Inscape* (*Journal of British Assoc. of Art Therapists* Spring 1989. David MacLagan)

The time of th writing includes 4 partys: the end of Film Festival party, th Wide Angle party, New Decade party, & my birthday party.

# Letter from the Takeaway

Dear Thomas

If youve notisd poets introduce ther poem, lyk they want ye to locate it in som special mood or circumstans; & they do this genial preambl wher yore seeing them in ther best liht. & then ye hear ther vois change & you know theyr *reding*.

Wy is poetrie reiterating failur – That is the defincion. A lyf of purposelessness supported by state intervencion, redundanciez special register

state purpose a con text. Hav ye opend the fuckin shop yet. Declarativs bleeding all over th place

State bordom state

to an observor a clock slower prezent flashing thru th window, 'I' am serving, I serving, surprize palookas Old Hill,

restor servisabl bordom, misprizion to publish, orders from the cownterevolucionary masses

selfserviss howrs, interested 'I' resind aresting star, with system to will

takaway 'I', power flares in th kitchin, surpriz randomly orders at th counter, at th standing wave indeterminacy singly system

random heet in uprore a single partickle falls thru my solid state improvization, the system hole.

Surprising spases order the flash fyre. Willess riting orders willess films twitter in the emulsion, fag ash flake in th career bordom: sifting lung, radiat waveforms passing thru fresh ayr.

Ye dunno whar im fuckin on about doo ye – howdya lyk to be a director in an Indian takaway

Consiousnes falling thru space, binary sistems filling pages, fractal orderz flaring into univers the witless purpos, 'I' cd be a director

fractal metafors rebownd to mindz simulacrum, riting anti riting

Ar the particles hurting yoo – Is th shit falling thru yor belly

If ye lern harmonicks by distributing ball berings on a pool table, the way Pythagoras iniciated into the hier dimensionz & forswor beens, yoo wil discover how the univers flows.

Now lets just unpick this shal we – yoo want to be a restauranteer. Riht. Or a computer operator. Riht.

Cancerus cell mutacions in the bladder of my lovd one. I hav work to do. Unfortunatly her marrige is no wors than myne.

Pulses stor energy. Spiritual consentrates. The system cannot sustaiyn motion, the atoms heet loss setle to dissolucion, bodies transmigrate to the cold soop – the strong force flor sustaiyn th body - rearrange the molecular balans of yor futur!

The fractal metafor sustaining poop, entropick conseits curry modernist expreshions meeningles outlets.

Lets examin this shal we – th gramar-generating failurs, efortless diarrhea from grammars distribucion curve

Letter from the Takaway whirling in the chaos responding flow

one poet vainly trying to rite poetrie
? the commoditiless spaces

atoms going bananas!

State purpos a beleef statement. I keep seeing theez fucking litle pollen seeds dansing in th solucion statistical faith

*Whad is dis. Hehh. Yoo nadder mentall wan. Him in kitchin alredy mental toking hizself – I tawt yoo litel orrite but now, hi see yoou nader mentel wan –*

*What yu rite it. Oriht my frend, we wil see, jast well see –* order constativ in gaps –

automatizm articls defalt, misprizion escape onlie referent its internal set,

a relaxing of will probabilitiz abownd wher reeders of th menu work harder than th waiter

th smaller the extant material from the original fryup th grater privelige conshiusness in the prick of spase

yoo are catshit on my shoe. I hav spent 20 yers getting ware I am today. Jeezus.

*Whad is dis, rabbish heh. Still is mind like beforr.*

*Yoo tinking lyk bifore wan – Yah yu dreeming. Neverr be… Okeh, well see. Farst making money uknow, farst yoo larn it to stend. Dont tinking yu meking me favore unow – we can help eche oder – I can help yoo – ya, estru.*

*I want to make yor mind diffrant –*

*Jast we open resturant ynow, jass is see what heppen.*

*I want to myke yu good waitering, yenow. Forget dis beforr wan. Yoo nebber be no. Yoo tink yu ar mebbe wan day big riter – iz never be - owr peeple dey nevar allow –*

Publish the compleet body of inertia.

*Farst heb to be rich! Yah i kno dis – iss tru. I mek estudy yewno. Not lyk us foor.* This is obviusly corect. Its the access to noble thawhts – i alwys thoht peple wer obligd to see th holines of the Buddha or St Francis – otherwiz it wud hav bin embarasing

pathological abnegacioun taking social form – cors now ye can go bakpacking

*So yoo larn it waiytering ynow – I want yoo larn it – yoo war flimmakar but yoo can be waitering not too late –*

*You can change – yah I belieeb!. Men can change it hiz liyf.*

*But yoo hep to kno how to sarve cashtomer. Jus make dem heppy.*

*Birmingham 1994*

# Second Letter from the Takeaway

Deep personal unhappness is not a good start. How abowt
mild malaize. Subsuming ideologs rancid litle fuckups.

Deep personal conviction is never enow to make a curry.
What we need is a job. Its nobody elses falt.

But also 'I' az an incomprehensible large part of th known
univers. Everytime I look it fills it.

Cries fall from the page, iniquitus structures seep into
prosody

poetry atracts the suffering fool, wile others program
interactiv softwaer I am red

Now then wher are we. I have got somwaere & Im no
further than i started

We analyze from fundamental to randomness becuze its
convenient. But in an infinitly extendable univers any point
is an arbitrary set of relacions we alwayz find ourselvs in th
midle of

but somwhere in this vector between Halesowen & Cradley
Heath transendent meaning: sucsess

Wat we cal our lives arbitrary convencions establishd for
habitual modes of perception –

my producers let me down. Ive forgoten how old i am.
Im overqualified az a secretary. Its too interesting to get an
erection. Im living w/ my mom. I see haf an howr of daylite.

Its dificult for relacions not to form in hyperspacial axes all concevable structurs

my life, as the saying gos, is compozd of thez tetrahedrons cubes octahedrons dodecahedrons icosahedrons rotated

Do yu understand me too wel. Do yu understand me too well. Ye fuckin dont yknow.

I got my langwage from TB Pawlicki. In the spirit of a raving sawcer paranoiack & dispassionat ironist of the new phyzics.

Its so exsiting purposiv discors wich beleves it is not abowt discours conceets it refers to somthing, escape onlie referent

Wen sciens becoms pathological it iz poetry as far as it is sciens – reding stochastick purpos into universal deluzion. Show us eny object or poeisis to rezist *Why yoo rite it dis*

A nife a tinopener a Chicken Tikka a customer all legitimatly asking *Whad is dis – Hey fool – yoo lezy boggar ynow. Yoo shud be sarve cashtomer yknow not reding book. Yu shud not be siting wen cushtomer gib order –*

Wen a standing wave patern is acselerated to the velocity of th radiant waves wich create it, its 3 dimensional structure disapears altogether

Im going to kick his fuckin hed in.

It is an awkward transicion from aggresiv sexuality of th criminal underclas to a Tory Cabinet minister. Thats why impotens is important.

*Hey i told yoo bring this shit book, yu jas doing nathing reeding blady book, i tol yoo don bring dis – yoo focking lazy boggar jus reading book*

*yoo jus wark for maney yuno – yoo nebber want to be muslim – I want to mak ewe good waiter but yu never lissen, yu jus wark for my money – yu Inglish craftie peple ykno*

*Yeh – yeare not white yoo ar gipsie mongrel – yoo Cristian peple craftie boggar yuno*

*Yu ar fly ewe ar not human even, yoo fly – I kill yu yoo fuckin shit man – I kil yoo yu cunt – if wan kick i braek yor hed yukno – yoo Chrishtian fucking, yoos peple Cristian fuckin rarz clat, I not going to pay yu wazes – yeah, y/ neber wark Friday – I not gibbing it yu wazes –*

The chickin is alwayz vibrating to random moleculer agitacion of heet (as far az th chicken is consernd the extra vibracioun it gets from being pluckt is just mor heet) *yoo fark off man, fark off owt of my shop – yeah – yoo warking for my wages & yoo geting labour yah – I tel socell securitie – yoo wil not get wages*

*yoo peple wil go to hell – yoo shit man yu fockin barstard – yu make oders suffering – yoo tink yu are make them heppy – ewe arsk them. Yoo fuckin Chrishtian yor mother she make yu barstard – barstard fock – get get out – yoo wil punish – for tree generation – yore fucking Hakim family wil go to Hell – yore fuckin Hakim yor father he shit he mak barstard Christian*

*yore sishter dey Crishtian, I see yore sishter yeh width fuckin*
*Irish rabbish shit – yor sister dey go in street – i going to kill dat*
*old woman & that Hazi – I kill yore shit mahder – dont tell*
*her to pray she going to hell yeah – she going to hell – not laffing*

*yoo fock yir sishter das what make them Cishtian al of dem –*
*yoo hab sex wid yor sister – ew lisehn – yeh yoo heb sex*

*Birmingham 1994*

# Third Letter from the Takeaway

I keep dreming ive got a term project where ive never gon back to the class in months.

Yoo imagin inconseqwensial hermeticks abandoning th masses; you never interview anywon less than a rap gangsta, defens lawyer with a film deal, riting not narativ

In several yers nothing makes a diffrens. Animus ingested entropy remaines. Reserchers in a pharmaseutical discover a receptor for Republickanism in the brain.

Wher is it situated a poem impossibl to acsess. Experiens tels me noone wil giv a living riting word salads, I wudnt bet on riting not narative

but how do ye *kno* an audiens cant get it. Ive ever made judgments on behaf of peple.

A polemick of use value. Storiz setling unstably between textuality & inertia

eliptical poetries of a clozd univers, suckd back to th pointles event horizon of my arsehol:

I got my langwage from a sawcer loopy consummat stylist of th new phyzics. Its such a relief to find discours owtside of discorse, hyperbolick retoricks of openess held in check by engineering

altho matter everywere pul on it, spred thin enufh so that it wil never collaps back onto anything important

'I' as emergent phenomenon, imperial syntax – yor emergent behaviour w/ time they al fade toward invizibility, ther shop sine radiacion geting weker & weeker – the parabolick bearly making it to infinity befor exhawsting kinetic energy, to end as a tandoori cinder

declarativs of the new natur, omniscient descriptiv of a universal discors nowon knos wat theyr tawking about

geometrick waves dizolving ripple molds on the clozd I

the order of development, zygotes pulsing, genoms turning eche other on & off on the bullion network

eche lihtbulb connected to 2 others switching faster than liht chasing informasion beyond the 'C' of relativitie in a cyberloop flying sauser

antichaos boxes its possibilitees into a tiny range as shit fals on the shitpile model, landslides bild to stabl states, to periodic tectonick colapse, we only hav won pile of shit afeckting eny part of th pile

systems permanent wobble between redundancie & automatizm, grammar pressurs default

an expected property of mathematical chemicals

proze autocatalytic sets, intrinsic dynamicks of probubble structur

celular automata dying, expanding paradym loops from a sentral region ded tree – expanding *what*?

ther ar only 2 rules – Reproduce – Mutate

the parasites take advantige of information, others take advantage of th parasites, & others cheet on society, wether chemistri of carbon & hydrogen, or the computer bits simulacion of Hegelian society

logickless currency fluctuacions of democratick capitalizm, the end of th best of worlds – the prosodic tools predictiv power

look for paterns & price fluctuacion, understand L=A=N=G=W=I=G=E poeticks, make a fortune on stocks & shaers

eny ecosystem exists at khaos antikhaos –

whas a chronometer – 2 snails placd on a copper plate forever in sympathetik communicasion

the oscilating energy of sparks as electromagnetick waves as lipodes spred owt on a pond

whoever hears it coms into tune, the amplitud is magnifiyd

The Hertz transcever acros a tiny gap iz this letter, mor vigorus sparks of a sensless devise

wave a white handkerchief ech time the recever experiment fail

litle I, th valorizd underclas in college, trying to rite the cliche & unspekable

O Planet of the Lower Classes

ware litle white daddyz girls opress the blak studs – now *hoo* am
i thinking of ther

suppresst in liberal storiz of essentialist conflict

empowerment by predacion – *Stab up me meat, boy, stab up
me meat*

batty bwoys getting ther hed mashd in by gobshite w/ hihly
developd sense of black potency, & blordclaat sociology

*I dont speke worrd a man – dis sey I must mooltiplie, an mankind
unto mankind is an abominacion heh heh heh*

political definicions pop – all Black peple ar interreplasable,
therfore I only need one homogeneus black blob


The desert iland test of the ontogenetick.

Langwige defining geografies waer the universals of anthropologie
play owt the constant oposition – defining 'selfhood' in th tribe,
the conservativ economy of identitie


Oh God – Im a racist! God, wharra *releef.*


at $10^{-43}$ second, temperatur a funcsion of overcrowding $10^{32}$
degrees, the 4 nown forcez of aire fyre curry powder & water
wer one

the *eliptical* model poem has a begining end a liftime. Gravi-
tacional redundansy is relentless. Its contents ar destind to fry.

*Birmingham/London 1994*

# Fourth Letter from the Takeaway

If I blew a hole in th roof of a mooving carrige, the shell wud
crash thru th same roof on return – we hav horizontal mocion,
& the aire is not snatcht away

lerning coms when yoo hav to stay when ye dont want to; th
flow of events on tracks, apointments kept for faild careers not
riyting

moovment acros tectonick feelds, folded geologiez, all energy
burns angular movement owt of the inertial momentum

Serbs & Croats holding liynes of interracial identitie over
centuriz, nocking lumps out of eche other transmute feral
energy; any 2 particlz attracion the product of thaer mass –

*The Prezident got shot in the buttock! – (We must shoot him in a
part of th body thats mor politicaly advantageus)*

the objectshaping subject

pulld into a fanshape zoom along the line of tyme, the imige of
bird in meditativ platitude

at the riht angel flow, won horizontal monoplainz snow,
ilustrated on surface lyk a polygraf page

military aplicasions mimick theempark riydes: hydrolick & visual sync, persistans of inner ear freefall, eye redes one thing, body another, & travel sickness simulacion w/ yr own 3-D sickbag

Wat is unhappiness – a fleeting fickle, a housewyf wavelenth, murder by personal columms, statistickal analyseze for serial rape in cort – a thawht or fragment memorie becoms reality & to rite it down maks it real

frustrated black executivs sit in virtual suits mugging little old ladiez & declaring in refined tones, Take that, you mizerable honkey momma!

A crie for a last lyf, an examination of experimental vacuitiez: the train of disconnection wich linkt the particlz of determinizm, th laws of nonlinearity the historical battel between parasience & humanitie, a last qualificasion;

refind & verifyd bias a last qualificasion for the unemployabel for a lost autodydact.

It coms, it goez. It comes it goz. Personality on th busride, genitiv neural pathway

softwaer astrologikal progressions foretell yoo will shortly be charged £50 reeding fee.

In asynchronus futur, astrologikal computer reedowts begin to reveal congruent blips, a distant end. The sad representativs of parasience – financial oraculs to multinacionals futurz too short term to register – get the acsidental indicaters of general catastrofhe from indivijual cases. The bullion market is strong till total freefall. As tyme gos by, deth has a recurrant date.

plazma vorticis coming down creating corn crop siyns

insident liht drops off th buswindow, the intersecions of interior lyricizm & photons redistribut an imige world

waer doz the mirrar wirld exist if an elektron is nockt off the greese, is ther a simpl dimension of poiynt by point reproducsion, a perfect reflective plane acuity?

waere did all the antimatter go – in som mathmatiks?

the ability to see th wondering is to place the wirld on 2 dimensions, owt of th relacional;

If yore not sure, best use a poeticks that isnt sure; its this conviction, a riting isnt inabilitie, angwish isnt banal

evvry water molecule in th body saying Give me particulate polutants, giv me flu

Dr Radovan Karadzic new the unrealitie of th peple – mor important for the curry than th lives they scrabble after; the tru artist, bore screems as the skulptor bears th chips from th beten stone, blud & breth elements undergoing chang to fuel radians

sociyetiz in wich incresing numbers ar living in th rong dimension, peple infatuated w/ disatisfacsion, th wimens selfhelp industry. Need expands to fill tyme. Th horizon forever receding to fill unhapines

but wen peeple are igniting th fyres of racionalizm, if it wasnt Kalashnikov it wood be an ax

the tilted balistick picking up kinetick energi. Twisting on its axis, taring mussel ligament clothing, ricocheying bone entering & reentering on its spiral & nowone knows wher its going to cume out –

fiyting torq, spectral fetures redshifting the fuck out of here, a gravitas of revolucionary speed, we shud all be geting screwd into the grownd. Hey, Im gerring screwed into the ground!

It appears Im thin – wich is to behave as liht – squeezing in the direcsion of velocity. O Barnet Newman zip, O clock slower region – a face presst aginst th glass of th spaseship Old Hill Indian Takeaway

I made a choyse, & it made me. & this seems to me a nontrivial unscientifik truth.

Rejecting major religions for a thozand tiny gesturs & beleefs of personal energi. A futur orthodoxy of pluralist New Age gibberish; gravitate to clozd system

The Judeo-Christian religions acurate to w/in a factor of 5.

*I was raped by electromagnetik disturbanses,* hypersensitivitee to elektromagnetic polution at fawlt line hotspots –

unlawful noledge by an alien w/out a proper passport, w/out recorse to counseling except a polygrafh test –

*They shone lihtes in ma face & a unncanny wayling noiz issud frum ther spasecraft wich wuz lake whirling w/ colurrd lahts. They wer kinda lake human beens cept of they was larrger than us & balloon shapd & held together roun thayr middle baa utility belts. They wer communicayting w/ ther mothership, I herd em say on theyr communicator they had a situacion going on, & then they proceeded to examin me by takin daan ma pants an inserting a probe up my posterior.*

*& wale theyr like sientifick reserch was stil in progres, I did ask if they wer goin to be don soon, but then wun of the alien numbers took owt a long lazer wepon – it was abowt 3 feet & smooth & sylindrical – & he pistol whippt me w/ that som.*

*When ah came to I was alone in my bed but ah still had wun of the aliuns sahntific instraments jammed in my rectum. Yes sir, I had th doctor remoove the instrament – it looks lak a short rubbery tube object an its capabel of emitting a liht beem – we beleve its a dematerialazer or a radar scanner of sum sort – & we fownd som Ever Redy battries inside.*

---

The examinacions included: NVQ III Informacion Tecknologie (City & Gilds 1994); GCSE Mathmaticks Grade C (SEG Summer 1995); GCSE Physicks Grade D (MEG June 1995)

The text books included: Physicks for GCSE (B Johnston)

I was in pre-producsion for a film, otherwiz id hav had much better grades for Maths & Fyzics

# Letter to Peter Gidal/Kurt Kren

Dear Mr Gidal

Ive only seen one of yor films – ther was a girl in a room
&, dare i say it, not a lot happend. I use to hav neg rushes
coming out of the Coop printer w/ th skie bleched owt like
that & Id just dump it.

So im not sure how y/ relate to my pm, except y/ serve as an
analog for som characterizasion or expresivity, a duble, to be
projected into.

I supose the poetick as epistel in insult, w/ a performativ
undecidabiliti is in my working praxis of sociel producsion,
rather than pms as shiny packiged commodity. Or not so
shiny chapbook tat. Use valuw over som kind of surplus
mental labar.

& yet i want works, I think Mikhel Palmer was saying about
– pomes so comfortabel in thir assumpsions, of transparensy,
they can be red w/ slack atencion waiting for a bus. Pms
seeming to exist to relate som epifhany on the bus frm riter
to reeder.

W/ varyus photos of me on th dust jacket, participating in
the optical illujion of the 1st person: lyke the editers even
distrust the I of th poem & haf to reinfors th fals realizm by
having 'real' peeple stareing bak at the reeder.

Oh no Mr Gidal, is this a 'voyce' pome. I must be a bad
person. I must rite out a thosand tymes I must fractur th
dominant codes of 1st person discours.

As i seek to repare the distorcions of split kulturs, ethicks & estheticks of marginaliti drawing the sutably fucktup together; the colapse of communizm & Bank of Credit & Commers under the wayt of ther own illigitimasy:

so i emerj into new alienacions: th trace of body & damige the modernist project antagonizm, & the commonality of narrativ waere the familie can see, & cover, itself.

Mind yoo, Mr Gidal, i did sume performans pms w/ lik a forgrunding of Realizm, one where naturalism overwhelms w/ no formalist element – do you wanna hear th one abowt my haercut?

*i hadn't had a harecut in lyk ages & it had just grown out of whatever 60s 70s Lady of the Lake styl & into Wild Bill Hickok. So i goo inside & say Giv me a girls harecut. Well hav a look thru this she seys & tosses me this manuel of wat the girls wd be waring & mister I was just wreckkt from th distans between thez mothwatering creacions & th greesy tat –*

No? Yre proberly rihte.

Anyway I was at this S. Asian Nacional Arts Stratagy conferens in Burmingham, its ware i first met Atif hed come up for his dissertasion, & i wus payd to go w/ my sister for BCMA. It was lik all filld w/ arts buracrats;

the conformist ranks of western cultur as the vangard of the political strugle: if we can create a multidepartmental comunity who hav no idea ther is a chipshop owtsyde

By the way Atif – when did Cultural theorists deside I was Black? My mom, & my cusins in Mile End they stil dont know theyr Black & coopted into th Struggle. Theyr still waiting for a Counsil house if theyre lissening. Im happy to be coopted by progressiv intelectuals, but cud i possibly be calld Tea Colored? I lyk it qwite stroong.

Restructur the hierarkies of curating & exhabicon, & i am the perfect person to fill that project.

Bring me the ordinarie lumpen boorjwazie to reprogram;

& this chair, Jagbinder Lhamba or somthing, was doing his mantra every so often lik, when he was going on abot underepresentasion in administrativ arts qwangos, & support for Blak arts strategick blah blah –

& hed be going *Of corse this cuntry is racist. This is a racist administracsion.*

Hes rihte! My category! My Black and Minority Ethnik shopping trolly! We are innosent!

What does Racist society mene, ware the legislacion for industrial discriminascion, Eqwal Opportunitis, Govt wite papers, all party recomendasions, gidelines for scools, armd forces, police, reserch on over-representacion in mental helth care; wen th statefunded legislasion & academic papers wd bury Balsal Heeth.

O Grate wite theorist. In wat context is it racist. In relacion to the pictur in his hed. Shd we compair the papermontain from this contry to India, or Guyana, or China. & doz the amont of legislatur proove racizm if its vast, or absent.

This is a racist cuntrie… in relacion to what, Disneyland. & what bit is. The contrie as selfexisting rayificasion as oposed to us lot. Wich peple. Doz that include blak peeple. Do wee

have a stake in this construcsion. Or ar we just the Good
others in som kind of ontogenetik priority & were not in
*This is a racist cuntry*. Weve only been here 50 yers we dont
make societi. Good old Jagbinder calling to ritual book
the arts oficers from Regianal Arts Bords, & managers of
cultural gilt – my niggah!

Well Mr Gidal, Atif is now chair of the Bord at the London
Filmmakers Co-op, that marvelus throwbak to the Cultural
Revolucion, now singelhandedly holding bak the tide of th
mixt economi, refuzing the neutralizing clayms of television
& sponsership, & insisting on the artists rite to make films
w/ Lottery money.

I shd inform yu in the spirit of openness, that both Atif & P
have dubius status in that upstanding institusion, freqwently
lamenting th lack of good looking Bunnies at the Coop.
I am sorry to say that sins yr tyme it has been swampd by
unrepresentativ coons. Insidentally I kno y/ were concernd
at the underrepresentacion in Executiv & Workshop by
wimen, now hapily redressd by a cell of lesbians. However,
acording to P, as many seem in the proces of having sex
changes, ther is litel room for complacensy in owr gender
eqwality stratagees.

I spek to my funders & colege lecturers who dominat S&M
clubs – straws ar inserted into nostrils in the masking tape
clamp reveiling exquisit judgment were the fear parcel
sufocate – to the celler drible tapes

intervensionist pietizms in the artworld, sustayn th bulemic
& marxian victim –

Sing: rezistant is better

Im gonna do another party pome – its a weltrodden genre of myne, other peepal retire into naturs depopulated solipsizm, i invent enconters of excess.

Dere Atif, I cam down for yor party at Cavendish St. This poetick trajectori of significant experiens – a poetrie of personaliti that exausts itself exacly whare the pesonality is exausted. So me & yoo & Leandro & hippy Richard go off to som students halls at 4 or 5 & Leandro sells us som acid, & honestly i cd hardly fucking focus over th pool table for drink – & this wired preshure in my groyn.

OK we stumble out som tiym in th morning & yre babbling how th sky looks so fresh – i thoht it was just some socializd delusion – like its alwys been fresh. Dont start coming over visionary cuse the kemicals firing off the neurons for poetry or somthing.

& we find this hidden Jos cafe – whare was it Atif – ive fucking forgoten. Ware was the colege. So we went to th cafe on our way bak. Dye remember. Ariht. & we had a cookd brekfast ther & lik – I alwys thoht id lernt the langwage of categoriz lik i lerned karate, cuse i use to try & explain ideas but it never cohered.

But i was trying to explayn my reservacions to Leandro & Richard about – i cant remember – like they mite be going on abot the Criminal Justis… no, th Poll Tax – & the repressions of varius local goverments, & i had this mystical take that i didnt beleve in evil men syndikated tyranniz controling producsion & th menes to understanding this power monopoly;

I dont hav a real knoledge of th money supply or sewers under our feet & how Lambath Counsil can actuly operate

given the theeving baboons they put in plase; & that
ordering on maybe som instinctual level becoz of our
langwige wired social predisposision has mor often than not
com up w/ hierarkic structurs that God didnt care abowt.

& i was burbling that peple create these forms, & th terible
thing is that lifes morr interesting than Marcuse.

They probably thowt it was the LSD – & ther i was just as
retarded as ever. & they waz saying – well actuly they were
extremly skeptical – Richard waz saying that, No he cud Feel
the represhions of state as instituted by legislasion… but they
were fair – I mene they listend to me.

Dere Mr Gidal,

we go bak to Cavendish St this icy morning, just lolling at
Atifs after th party, I get realy interested in th thred patern
on th futon duvey. Leandro ses wile im playing chess w/
Richard that i sudenly look selfconfident, not like when we
wer owt, Cool is th word he uzd. He probly saw this goofy
litle person gon silly w/ drink & frail in th wind. All v.
interesting Mr Gidal – i never saw that. Look, im geting to
it, im geting to it –

Cauz thoze lot, they bin planning sins the other day to go
to this Remembranse day demo, err, the BNP wanted to do
this march on Whitehall wherever, & lay a wreeth, & i think
Leandro & Richard ar old hands, & Atif – he was fucking
up lik a kite for it, he wanted aggro, hed bin telling thes
lurid storiz out on sume frontlin confrontasion the other day
hadnt ye Atif – dye member – yu went w/ yr camera. I wasnt
that keen but suddenly like 10 or 11 in the morning & peple

are *wired* & we wer on our way to Victoria Sq, me feeling all
spindly in th biting wind & eazily led by radical discors.

I was not looking forward to this back to th 70s clash
between th forces of the Good Class war & the poor old
factory fodder racists from Poplar & Dagenham. Ther was
all this kind of good fiht antagonizm energy lik they knew
who the enemy was. & i just new they wer goin to get me
into wone of thez runing skirmishes waere ither the police or
som bomberjacketed fattys wud kick me to fuck.

If y/ go to Victoria St, just owt of th tube & the bus stacion,
& thers this triangular island – & ther was alredy a cordon
of polece & this particuler activist party – who werre they
Atif. & lyk we duck under th cordon not realy nowing wat
was up, when it was hapening. I gorra tell ye, the entire tyme
of this stint on the baricades – the onlie thing the acid was
doing i swore blind that snow was falling blown onto my
muth. & i kept brushing thes cold flakes away – for hrs.
& also – Im not sure i shd include any of this – im not sur
about any of this storiez impeding or retarding devices to
atension –

this examinasion of mening, is somthing ignord this prosodick
units, the unexamind transparent life waffle; a riter skimming
for perverse rezons, th sort of confeshional remorslesly aserting
its awthenticity in flat declarativ sentencis

I imagind my ex was w/ me as we stood bewilderd, I think
Atif had no idea wat was going on as the cordon becam a
semi legal embargo & nowone was alowed to leve this knot
of 60 or 80, & th polis cordon ronde it becam rigid –

& like thru the hrs, ware this was supposd to be a meeting
poynt to go onto th rumble, it becam this ritual performativ,

bashfuly pushing agenst th cops & chanting pig slogans when y/ didnt feel they were teking it personaly – the cops had a tactic under wat bylaw i dont know, that they wernt going to let us moove.

I say us. The good thing abot the entirly expository, & incapabel of metaforical thawht, is – I lookt at theez – who werre they Atif – & they were the most diseazed runtish looking motley. I mene child sycologists tawk abote a depresingly familier apearans of thes damigd neglected abused children, who look the unloved bone;

my ex she was always so dismisive of my loozer frends. & i cd just imagin it, weed be standing ther wispering, *Oh my God, weve ended up w/ them – were protest lozers.*

Is this the fascistick gaze. I think its a look that is freed frm humanism.

O Kurt Kren – yoo shud be heare to film this shambles & turn it into a Mensa test of structurd flash frames

We are exhorted by th Workers Party chain gang leder with encommiums to the sucsess of our demo – if shes going to lie to her own cannon fodder yu know shes the rihte man for the Party.

on the other side of the cordon a BNP leader is doing an elegie to the Humanitis department colonized by zombie bulldykes who cut th balls off the opresser lecturers – so heroick, so lost, I want to fly to the hopeles cauz

I think sombody spiked th snowflakes & were all having a mass halucinacion a strugle session in th kettel –

waere the poliese put the yung woman in a stress posicion
holding a riot sheeld behind her bak – who thinks its part of
her student techer training

we tare off our cloz in the recuring senario of the rabble Picts
agaynst Roman *testudo* – me swatting th snow flurriez off my
face –

& it turns into Wienner Aktionismus – I dont now if weere
trying to pelt th pigs as they squeez us but we get coverd in
wedding cake floure sheeps blood & sumwone urinats on a
strangley excited constabul, but weell blame th pigs


illocusionary acts stating fact exibiting anatomical spesimen
or engaging in erotick display

Dear Kurt Kren

what did Otto Muehl think of yor documentasion of his
staging of sado myzogynist Aktionism – you turnd his
lunatick food rape into a metonymy of body parts iterated
into indiferens.

The Truama story

ther was pussy food animal guts flowers & a shit pool
sucking the liberal scapgotes into the artists post-Auscwitsch
fat reservoir: & the star of th show was – yorr horizontal
splice ripping th flash frames.

Yoo sertanly fuckt him up Mr Kren.

Whats it liyk in the afterlyf Mr Kren. I red you lost yr job at th bank. I met a yung man at Anthology Arkives who use to hang owt w/ yu wherever yu wer dossing at th tyme Hooston maybe – & he sed you never spoke abot yr work yud just drink beer together & wach th football. Is it tru yu ar the [Anton Webern/Gottfreed Benn/Kurt Kren] of Uropean experimental film?

I wonder if yud have filmed one of my performans pms. Do you want to heare the one abot my shoos? *This wone was when i was siting in Ravels w/ won foot in my messy pece of Kung Fu sliper & the other foot in this work of art lyk my riht foots saying This is th past this is the rubbish of yr life, & my left foots saying Heres swishnes heres a sex operacion heres –*

No? I got a hundred mor lyk that…

Anyway were all showting showting – well *theyre* shouting, im hoping the coppers keep me kettled – the Workers Party gang leeder is on her megahorn: *O belevers! stay firm in th face of the most apalling falsificasions. All women hav the riht to an abortion a free baby & a handgun!*

Were all going to the Friedrichshof commune – ware thers shugar plum trees & lemonade fountins & all the eclairs yoo can eat & yoo never have to go to school agen & we can throw off th mind shackels of the Reich & sine up to have wild legaly binding foreplayless drudgery – under the benin rule of a priapik garden gnome

O to be a gullable pece of meat! O to be yr shit!

My Texas Chainsaw family

the Pied Piper struck up & th throng folowed irresistably –

yoo heroick vangardists – smash th bawbles of love, the
ilusory onepointednes, stop the delusional endorfhins in
female brains, & flatten sex into a feeturless orchard of
bodiez,

we browsing sauvages
we fluid feudal lords!
we soft obliging serfs!

in the fatherles creshe thers an endless supply of [proteen/
futur sex/diarrhea/] love

Dere Mr Gidal

is this wat drove us into the minuted bord meetings of th
Film Coop.

never again wil we film anything vagely interesting, deniers
as we ar of the Antagonist – a paralyzing politicyzation of
the body that becoms so untenable its mor or less haram.
& polemicks aginst narativ that impels a movment from
a posision in a social spase of social menings or a politikal
spas – to & into a diferent human residens – another body
or figur – wher the phantazms & fantasiz, th realitiez of
projeccions, ar enacted.

Wat do yu think about this pm Mr Gidal – an object sutably
dulld & banal, lik the cuniform tablets of shipping invoises
& civil disputs

Oh Mr Gidal, all I had to do w/ my thozand feet of 16mm garbige – Id wait at the other end of th dryer as th leeder came out to find wat I alredy new: that it was th rong apertur, or this one time Id switched the lenzes over on the Bolex during a shot only to see ther wasnt a lens over the actual gate. All thoze flickering grey feet – I cd have edited them into materialist oblivion.

Is this my choice – bitween a talky intelectualizm from the Himalayas of asceticizm that will get me a lecturing job –

or a media frendly subversivness that finds ample excews to get fitlooking birds to tak thir kit off & invites all the audiens to th backstage party?

O no, Im Kurt Kren

*London 1996/2018*

# Ben-Hur

Dear B

Do you remember wen I ran to Stockwel or Brixton tube to catch y/ bifore yoo disapeared to say *I do love yoo.*

Perhaps yr superier brittelnes & my superier horsshit wil alwayz get in th way. Evrything is fin if we tawk abot the England cricket teme.

I dont kno if im riting this 2000 yers ago – I wish y/ cd forget.

But I did catch yu up & y/ understood

our diferent tradicions hypostasized as Poesy: the rize of the middleclases & hysteria.

Did I tell yu th storie I told Reds & owr cuzins. Y/ kno how they wd mythologize my brekfast – no actuelly I wud mythologiz it for em.

I, Judah Ben Hur colecting comunity memory as isolated bed sors.

This WPC tekkin my statement wile the paramedicks ar sticking him on a stretcher & shes woried im spasd out. Id probably shoplifted somthing.

I was in this Camden charity shop & theze 2 goyim are having a set-to on th steeming Hiy St, & the sqwat ponytail goy daring this shwartz, lyk – *Make yer moove – Com on then...* I thawt th Nubian bloke was interfering with his car.

The ponytail coms in, all chuffd & ses *Hes a pervert.* I says
Wot. He seys – *hes using a mirrer to look up wimens dresses.*
Ten minits later th schwarz coms in & hes saying *So ya think
yer hard yeah*, & hez holding this brown paper bag handle
thing wich I think is th ladys miror, the empiricist metafors
alibi. & i gos behind him to I dunno, get in if it starts.

Al hell braks loose the glass lamps & ornaments, its raining
shards the Nubians thrusting *thuk thup* & ponytails
throwing punches & they get in this clinch. I jump on his
back & hawl him off & i dont kno he must hav sqwirm
out; the goy whos stabd lungez over me & falls over all th
shatterd bric a brak theyr chucking pots & vazes at eche
other.

Im folowing th Mamluk on Camden Hiyh St, i seys to th
Ponytail whos coming back, *Yoo stabbd*, & i see him holding
th plase. I folow the Mamluk thinking Im Famus Five.
Anyway he givs th slip on Greenland St Schmeenland St. Ive
bin heer befor, the yuneeq event wich maks meening thru
history, thru, becus.

Is that my lot – som banal urban awthenitissity? Im not
mekin another racist racionale soothsay.

A poem crys denial. O displasd comunitarians. O jihadless
jobless. From lyf without Royal Colege of Art to the life of
twiliyht press within. Waz, is ther, shal it. Egh?

(But our cuzins loved th story. Did I tell yu how I tole peple
in Bangladesh a slihte scar on my cheek was from a nife
fite. I think it was a bad shaving insident. But I beleved it
myself. Fufoo was saying I shud sort owt prayr duties as the
prospectiv child brides a strickly pius family)

I, Judah Ben-Hur went strait to th denotativ wich sed *I am pleazd* or *I am sorry.* & thers a feeling I slipt down a pasage of posible dimensions; ther wus the other spasetyme i opend th letter & clench a fist. Ther was a posibility the letters alter as aberacion of mind. The racionalist cognitiv senterd explanasions dont hold water when yore th Hero

mihty passions at boiling point & loud theatrickal tunes; think we missd th bote.

Brodcast engineers track narativs scope, rerite the descriptiv moovment disclozing the Word

the fatherless myth, reproducing anti Roman paradise. Fiht an idea with another idea! The ideology smashing superstructurs of plural poetriz!

Were ther is grate power, graet empire, grate feeling – error creeps in

the stone that fel from this room is still falling

not tears for the parents deth, but tears for speeches prohibicion; O lineal imperativ! O wifely unknown!

all acros the empire peple fite complecions family, clozurs marrige. Only I rite pulchritudes deceet. O line of softnes & conceet.

*It goz on – it goes on Judah – th race – is not – over...*

but lov them in the way they need to be lovd, as if yoo had never been heer

...

Deer B, I only had the haziest recolecksion of his fase. I tell ya wen i wen in to do the ID parade with the others, they cald me & my hart starts thumping liyk *I* wus gilty.

Luckily the goy with the ponytail told me hed trawld round in a polise car after he got owtta hospital & pointed him out at Camden Tube. So al I had to do waz pick owt the won closest to th story.

Th Kush barstard kept geting th trial put off for months. But when it got ther he was pleeding provocasion. He got 5 yers. His defendant got on me how exacly it started cauz wat I remember he started trashing th lamps befor he went for him, but I musta got it rong, whaddo I no –

We are th lost benefit seekers, we are all rowing a slavship to Syria – hoo knew 4000 *shahids* are stacking shopping trolleys wayting for a conflagracion of th hart.

My empiricist metafor is catching a traine to Birmingum – running to say *I do lov yoo*.

If Ben Hur can tuche his sister the leper…

Here is a coache of feeling. Therr is a coche of sadnes.

I dremed I cawt yoo in a bistro & i was in my dresing gown – its still 2000 yrs ago but set in the prezent.

Ther is retirment doggerel. A green spinster gable. A sadnes room.

*London 199(?) / 2018*

# Letter for S

Dear S

my Tomswood, damson sqwash pavements my girdeld
limits, yor seecret tarmac paths deluge bramble,

my cockt hat plantasion filld with boare, the barb roling nets
red & blackbrie – a finger gos down & plucks th hares &
bursting pods apart

my beares, lov tawht to eet th berries dirt

th plum delectabel distanse, th various tangle & stinging
buttonhole, & yor Brasher boots & a skirt for curious insect,
the sole scrunching unnown orderz

a little finger feel a firey apples bum, my lov tauht me bite
the green pimple, pressing th many grassis owr shirtskin

we lookd down at the cables & fantastick fescue ticks &
mites to share owr skin my lov, but I look for hymenoptera
th fairy flyz, the insect lover givz up to biytes

so much berry world, colour clots to who my lov – she
arguing for God & me arguing for the grasses, withowt baer
or deer, my wood hartbraking harvest

liht lowers & brings up hether wash, a faery tree, &
springing jeep ruts; paiynters painted liyhte in infinit
derivacion, & saw more stars & pantographs to plot th
growth of enclozure

evrywaere attendant brissles & sensilla scratch

but genre retired, & I never stood with an eazel looking at
nature like a prick

whaere do we go for low sensuousnes & delayd gratification
my lov; modernity screening owt projecsion sympathie
narrativ, sufferd me to underrite middleclass valuz

gave up conceptual prozodiz the good opinion of my peers,
how mimesis & temporizing plague the maker, & internet
porn, for yoo my lov

& craep leeves prinkt rust

I am leeding yoo a bearly ther path, wich coms of my
corupsion, & asking pathetick qwestions, I want you thair

buxom ruff roling to the edges of dark thickit, fructus & yor
old wood, yor dwindling integument & my late com

stripping diseazd skin, dig for bludy flowerd wolvz,

renewing landscap peepld lack, th waterfawling tree, th
rattling green, liyht is flowing thru & tyme is froing thru...

Hey lov, I cannot marry you for there is no use, I was
a postmodern clishe & cudnt liv th grate metanarrativ
of free libraris until I cum up agens the metanarative of
multiculturalizm

a demographick of aestheets becom sqwatters, or eqwally
schic drug uzers, but modern poetri chose them for its
sexless colorless brood, & I beleved them wen they didnt say
class was relevent

we joind you to have no money, no institucional capital,
& virtuous effacement; mothers aquird Welfar system

competens & broht us up alon, & I a partial subject have no meens to join the human race.

Yoo think if only I deliver yu fundamental meening weel eaze up & liv ever after –

(drop in a story abut sume peple goin – *Well I havnt red the er, but Im sure thers a diffrens bitween David Koraish & Jezus,*)

Its mor interesting than God. Also God isnt simple enouf. It is. It is not. It is –

But I'm in lufe with you – hey yoo!

gerrin drawn back to th limit for molten skyz molten God that poets tymelesly doo,

my autonomus relm, contaminated by nither kulture nor theery nor any fuckin houzing estats

how scool of Lorrain haz diffrent religius liyht to indiffrent Moneys – how my representacion of Lascauw as a lantern show is better than yorr exhibicion

but yoo can mak a diffrens. Yoo can decide this barbarick incizion is berrer than that barbarick infibulasion,

Thoz discriminasions, Miles, oh finicking surfaciz, warrisit they do! Sum politicks morr than langwage! I can sit at a table w/ five poets & cunnilinguas all rownd & noone can tell – sure that poetrie matters, oh I wish I cud, oh I wish I cud

descry thoz nonreturners riting water, whoz words disolve as soon as red & reform when yoo reed agen

& fell into noself to do the feeling, reducd to relacsionships
of overlapping, the paynted surfise becum the ethical plane

geting owt of my maids bed after the trifling Pimpernel
crying Oh, Master Champion – make me a good girl agen!

& chose immemorial logos,

But i'm in lufe with you – hey yoo –


Dear Andrew, yoo ever bin at a conference where a sociology
of poetries is denied yr own marginal poetics – bicause bad
ptry only can be analyzd but yorr practice needs only the
appreciasion of the good…Oh yeah, you hav –

I got on the British Poetris site yesterdy for th first time, to
have sprayd my sign in the pecking orders

the etiolacion, the dues – why didn I stick to wanking –

Andrew, I cant do it, I'm going bonkers w/ the metanarrative
of justice, & the world introjecting me up the ass. & those
small discriminacions –

am I a poet – or a poet. You remember th reding yu didnt go
to, & I wantid to do somthing with this. Some new register
– in a space

I'd been thinking about – I was in my Oxfam shop –
reprodusing th tape of Idi Amin intervewing hiz Bishop teling
his soldjers – Kickk him! Kickk him! Mek him crawwl!

But heere cumes the invazion of Tomswood Hill by refugees
with vengeful Gods & normativ sexeul relacions!

(Drop in th stori of th goverment oficial gets visited & the
oficer swings his 3 yer old kid by th feet & smashes his
brains owt on th wall; & then the tribal cheef who upset a
neiybour rival who cals the milicia – I hav a vaig pictur its
by a river or the vilage pool they meke him kill hiz six wives
& hiz children then hack his arms off on a ston & let him
crawl to Hospitle Hill to dictate this story –

Andrew, it was in my head, disruptiv to the edge of presense
agen, but heer it liys perfunctary an ded. Weer missing
an authenticitie of affidavit, an exhabicionist record the
experiens poem in th shop – but I *promiss* therz a way to
make it Hans Haacke

to be poetri & not poetre at th same tiyme) –


I waz a teenage teenajer, with authentick noselvs, but I red
it – morr aphid cookd in a sunfleck!

I waz a citie boy, filling hills with Welsh gorillas dying from
flu, & dirigible folly

bur I red it purple loosestrife & docks, so wele find it strange
jumping phasmida –

I am leeding you therr, & asking pathetick qwestions – Wat
was it like to liv at the end of th centurie az a subject of
poetrie – yoo viviparus wastrels…

but I'm in love with you – I'm in love with yoo – hey yoou!


*Ilford/London 1998*

Lightning Source UK Ltd.
Milton Keynes UK
UKHW011904300920
370812UK00002B/60